INSTRUMENTAL PASSION

INSPIRING WORDS BY THE MUSIC MAKERS IN MY LIFE

Instrumental Passion

CAROLYN ZEYTOONIAN

gorhamprinting.com/book/instrumental-passion

ISBN 979-8-218-22582-7

Library of Congress Control Number: 2023910915

Designed and printed by
Gorham Printing, Centralia, WA USA

For Alyssa & Oscar

I will be forever grateful for your unconditional and eternal love.

PHOTO CREDIT: ALYSSA FEDORCHAK

Oscar loved listening to Carolyn make music on her classical guitar.

Carolyn Zeytoonian

ACKNOWLEDGEMENTS

I WANT TO THANK my wonderful bestie and soul mate **Alyssa Fedorchak** whose pure love, enthusiasm and encouragement have been instrumental not only in the completion of this project but in my renewed passion for everyday life.

I also want to thank **Lauren Bateman**, founder and CEO of Lauren Bateman Music, Inc. She is a very special person in my life. When she hired me in 2017 to join her staff, I just knew that I would not only love *her* but would also love working *with* her. I am so grateful for the opportunities she has given me to become even more immersed in the magnificent world of music-making.

I am most grateful for the **Music Makers In My Life** who enthusiastically contributed to this book. Without them, there would *be* no book. I treasure their words of inspiration—and I thank them for sharing them with us.

A special thank you to **Kathy Campbell**, the creative and talented designer of Instrumental Passion, as well as the production team at **Gorham** who brought my music-makers' words of inspiration to life in this beautiful book.

If I am blessed with the opportunity to create an Instrumental Passion Volume II, I look forward to including the many amazing music makers who have entered and enhanced my life since the completion of this one.

Contents

INTRODUCTION

I AM BLESSED to have personally connected with so many passionate music-makers in my life. I admire their talent, creativity, and dedication to their art as well as their perseverance during the inevitable challenges that many artists typically face.

There are so many different reasons why people decide to make music. It's a deeply personal journey. However, the music makers in my life all have two things in common: a passion for making music and the willingness to share their experiences and inspiring words with you.

I wanted their words to all live together under the same literary roof. So I asked each of them if they would like to be included in my book which was originally intended to be a collection of inspiring 2- 3-line quotations about the role that music plays in their lives.

They were very excited about the idea and couldn't wait to share! Many asked about a word limit because they wanted to write so much more than a few lines! I certainly didn't want to cap their enthusiasm for sharing their passion for music-making or their words of inspiration and I therefore encouraged each of them to write as much as they'd like. Whatever it took to express what music-making means to them would be fine with me whether it be a short quotation, a few paragraphs or a 3,000-word essay.

And that's exactly what they did. They wrote quotations, aphorisms, mini-essays and longer essays. Some preferred an interview format while others wanted to tell stories. Their words were written specifically for this collection, for my book—simply because I asked.

I am just as grateful for the short quotations as I am for the longer essays. Each one is an inspirational gem. After all, *passion is instrumental* in making music. It comes from the soul—and its expression should not be capped by a word count limit!

While I do share a paragraph about how I met each music-maker, I did not include their biographies, list of accomplishments, contact information or website links—any of which could change at any time.

That would be an entirely different book and, most likely, a link-heavy e-book. I simply wanted to present, in their own words, what music means to them—and have those words be the focus on each page of an easy-to-hold hardcover book.

Whether you're already a musician or aspiring to be one, I hope that the musings of these fifty-seven music makers in my life will bring you closer to the reality of the human experience of making music. And if you simply enjoy books full of inspiration, may their words of passion, determination, strength and resilience give you a fresh perspective on your own goals in life.

. . . .

Carolyn Zeytoonian, Sales Director at Lauren Bateman Music, Inc., is a founding member and guitarist in Electric Thermostat, a Boston-based rock band. Making music with her precious guitars is her instrumental passion. She also loves spending time with her bestie Alyssa and Little Asher.

. . . .

LAUREN BATEMAN

Music is the truest form of time travel. It gives voice to the experiences in life you cannot describe and takes you back to the moments you've long forgotten.

—Lauren Bateman

Music was the voice that I never had. I grew up in a very strict Italian home. You were told what to do and you listened. Opinions weren't often welcomed and I was often made to feel like my thoughts and emotions were wrong. I learned to be silent, bottle things up and go stone cold to protect myself.

Then, I discovered music.

I always loved to sing but never made the choir and didn't make it into any talent shows growing up. My Mom enrolled me in piano and I hated it. But the turning point was when my sister bought me a guitar as a confirmation present when I was 16. I had been writing poetry in high school as an outlet for my feelings, but when I learned my first chords, I started writing songs.

It was exhilarating to put words to music. To feel the words and emotion moving in harmony with the chords. I was hooked. Since I wasted the piano lessons, no one was in a rush to get me guitar lessons. I had to learn on my own. And I taught myself strictly from the perspective of songwriting.

When I first started teaching guitar, I actually didn't know a lot of music outside my own. I had never really studied or learned anyone else's music. Teaching helped me become a better teacher, a better player and a better songwriter.

Music for me is one of the greatest gifts in my life. It helped me through so many tough times. Enough to write and record three albums and another that sits on the shelf waiting to see the light of day.

This is why I teach music to so many people around the world. Music heals. It transports us back to those memories long forgotten. It can get us through our darkest days and accompany us during our greatest moments. I believe that everyone should have the gift of music in their lives. It is why I continue to reach as many people as possible around the world. So that they, too, may experience the joy and happiness that music brings into our lives.

Lauren, founder and CEO of Lauren Bateman Music, Inc., has been instrumental in helping students of all ages become music makers. She teaches guitar to students worldwide via her online teaching platforms and YouTube. She is also the founder and owner of the award-winning LB Music School. I have been working with Lauren since 2017 and my respect and admiration for her just keep on growing year after year.

MARC ANGEL

Music is the universal language. The one thing in an instant that can change our mood or perception. Growing up, I was shy and did not fit in. I wasn't an athlete like the rest of the kids. I wanted something to make me feel important—finding a purpose or a way of expressing myself. Self-expression through a passion makes purpose. It gives energy, life, and love.

There is calm within the noise.

THERE IS CALM
WITHIN THE NOISE

Marc is a super-talented drummer who has been playing since he was 9 years old. I met Marc in 2015 when we were colleagues at PlayNetwork. We're on opposite coasts but, thanks to social media, we've followed each other's musical journeys and kept in touch over the years.

TED GIOIA

Ted and I have been online friends since 2016. A well-respected music historian, he's the author of 12 books including my favorite: "*The History of Jazz*". Ted is also the author of the *The Honest Broker*, a trustworthy guide to music, books, arts, media and culture on the Substack platform. I am so grateful to Ted for all that I have learned from him about music and their makers. When I asked him if he'd like to be included in my book, I was truly honored to receive his brilliant Aphorisms on Music.

Ted Gioia: Aphorisms on Music

Choosing your favorite musicians is like getting to pick your own parents. In a very real way you are now one of their descendants.

Long before the Internet, music served as a kind of cloud storage used by societies to preserve their most important information. Every knowledge vocation—medicine, ministry, philosophy, law, history, etc.—was originally practiced by musicians. When we treat songs as mere entertainment, we lose not only these traditions but much of music's inherent power.

If your music isn't changing your life, you've simply picked the wrong songs.

Songs are like fish and loaves in the miracle story—everyone who hears it can keep it, and it's still there for the next person.

What a great gift music is: It gives us satisfaction even before we're born, soothing us as we listen to the rhythm of our mother's heartbeat, and it's one of the few joys we can still experience in our final days.

Philosophers treat music as a kind of aesthetic experience, but it's more a physiological force. Long before a song impacts our ideas, it has already changed our bodies.

If I only get to bring one recording to a desert island, the lyrics better be about how to make a boat.

JOE ZEYTOONIAN

Hearing music that makes you crazy and that you love with all of your heart is a gift from the universe. Learn it, grow it and play it back to the universe with all your power.

—Joe Zeytoonian

Joe Zeytoonian certainly practices what he preaches. He is a world-class, award-winning oudist, singer, percussionist and composer and is music- and co-executive director of Harmonic Motion, which he co-founded with dancer and percussionist Myriam Eli. Last but never least, Joe is also my beloved cousin whom I have adored since I was a young girl.

JANE IRA BLOOM

I've been a raving fan of Grammy-winning soprano saxophonist Jane since the 1980s when I lived in NYC and saw her perform live. I wrote her a letter back then, letting her know how much I enjoyed her performance—and she wrote back to me! Those were the pre-email days of real letters on stationery! I was beyond thrilled. When I reached out to her and asked if she wanted to be included in my book, she sent me her poem "Hawk" that accompanied one of her trio releases with Mark Helias and Bobby Previte.

. . . .

HAWK

Spiral poets
    circle in three dimensions
        above melody,
            through time,
                under harmony
Speak to the air
    that holds its weight
        but never seen
Measure the ground and distance
        from the dirt
            in silence
Magnificent space painters
        blue singers,
            red bones,
                white hearts
Sky music makers
        without brushes
Invisible architects
        draw song, wing rhythm
            for as long as they can.

—Jane Ira Bloom

CHARLES MORTON

n grad school I studied pharmacokinetics, an obligatory over-syllabic word for how a drug, once it enters your body, finds its way into your bloodstream and then gets distributed to different organs and tissues at very different rates. Depending on whether you're talking about a shot or a pill, a dose given in the morning could be an immediate spike to the system that drops over time until the next dose, or it could be a gentle ramp up to a useful concentration before gradually wearing off until it needs a boost.

This era consumed my 20s, which meant I hadn't yet accepted the absurdity of my rockstar ambition. Most days saw me head from daytimes in lab to evenings in a dank rehearsal room where I'd plug a bass or a guitar into a series of pedals or rack-mounted processor units that I didn't really know how to use and twiddle these little knobs until getting just the right crunch and warmth and grit and however many other cliché musician adjectives you want to read in there before trying to capture my data in Pro Tools so that I could squint at the graphic waveforms and pretend to sound smart by saying things like "maybe we need to cut another dB of 1500Hz to smooth that out a bit, it's just so *aaaaangular* right now." Whether I had a bass slung over my shoulder or was sitting at the computer, I was frequently distracted by the results of that morning's series of experiments. Had I remembered to feed my cells? Did I leave samples in the scintillation counter or did I clean up after myself for once? Was the pressure on that column too high when I ran my chromatography?

Mercifully, our lab had a great stereo system that I unapologetically monopolized with mix CDs of stuff my colleagues hadn't heard of and frequently didn't want to hear again. Days comprised a lot of labeling of tiny tubes with fine-tipped Sharpies awaiting delivery of microliters of reagents during experiments tracking those drug molecules as they both moved around different biological compartments (maybe the cell cytoplasm, maybe the nucleus, probably the mitochondria—clearly the most \m/ METAL organelle). *You know what, maybe I should drop to A-minor in the bridge of that new song, that would really add some depth.* Sample time points to be taken at 30 minutes, 1 hour, 2 hours, get lunch, 4 hours, listen to last night's recordings, 6 hours, send out some emails begging booking agents for Tuesday night opening slots at clubs nobody goes to, 12 hours, 24 hours, wait what have I done I'm going to be here for days and miss rehearsal—maybe I'm going to have to take a hiatus from music.

When I did make it to rehearsal, I still had the concentration-versus-time profiles of multiple drug dose regimens floating through my brain, but they synched up very nicely with my guitarist's delay and reverb pedal settings. I knew that we could expect a dose to spike the drug up to a high level in the cancer cells we were trying to kill right after administration, and then gently FFFAAAAAaaaaaadddddeee... down to a sub-therapeutic level before we hit them with another dose, and if we got it right we could get an echo pattern that The Edge would appreciate—meaning we kept that drug molecule within a target range between efficacy and toxicity even though it had its rhythmic attack-and-decay behavior with every dose. Later, we studied multi-drug regimens to see if there would be a harmonious result from the administration of two different molecules, but this depended a great deal on sequencing: will two medicines sing in unison, or would call-and response make a better song? Are we giving too high of a dose for the system to respond predictably, or is the signal going to clip and distort—in ways that might be beneficial? Are we measuring the drug in the right compartment or should I move the microphone further from the cab and adjust for the delay later? Does it matter if we deliver the drug via pill, injection, or patch; or are we going to use the Les Paul for everything and see how it goes?

The mathematics governing my scientific and artistic lives were convergent, and that made me better and worse at both endeavors. And either way I was missing the point. Because every unique combination of fellow musicians to play with; friends trading mix tapes or mix CD-Rs or Spotify playlists; relationships where we have "our song"; total strangers also singing along to whatever awesome throwback track comes on the intercom at Trader Joe's—every instance where an overlap between the sonic orbitals around two people is revealed—is an opportunity for a bond to form. Part of my *brain* wants to transform every signal into frequency domain, point at the spectrum and say "A-HA, SCIENCE!", but by that point my *soul* has long since calculated the answer: we are wired to hear the connections in the universe around us, and we are blessed to get to communicate with each other via sound.

Charles Morton earned his PhD in Molecular and Systems Pharmacology and Toxicology in MIT's Department of Biological Engineering and since 2016 has served as a Lecturer in the Department of Chemistry at Brown University. However, the first thing I learned about Charles when he brought his children for music lessons several years ago at LB Music School was that he is a passionate music maker who plays bass guitar with some very cool bands. As you can see, he is also a talented and engaging writer!

KEN KALAJIAN

My first guitar was salvaged from our neighbor's trash barrel. It had only one string (low E) on it and the only song that I could play for weeks (by ear) was the then popular "Peter Gunn". After listening to this one song over and over again, my father looked at my mother and said that it was time to buy the other five strings.

As I reflect back on over sixty years of playing guitar with many talented and artistically diverse musicians, I believe that my greatest satisfaction was to see the joy that our performances brought to the audiences. My career began with a focus on Rock & Roll, mostly due to the Elvis Presley craze, which quickly grew to include both Middle Eastern and Classical music.

I was fortunate to perform with musicians who also embraced the many various musical genres that I enjoyed playing. As a long-time member of the Roger Krikorian Ensemble, our mission was to play exclusively for our audience, and not just for ourselves (great advice for young up-and-coming musicians). On and off stage, we had a strong and closely knit bond. We could feel the musical moves and direction in which the melody was taking us, but our goal was always to connect with the crowd. We were performing for them whether it was to celebrate our Armenian heritage or honor a family gathering. I have been blessed to uphold our cultural identity and hopefully pass this heritage on to future generations.

I thought of one more important piece of advice for younger musicians which I have taken from PT Barnum and used as my Golden Rule. "Always leave them wanting more". Like a short concise speech, a song should not drag on forever. Did you ever notice that the speech which gets the loudest applause is most often the shortest? After about 7 minutes you start losing your crowd. Very important strategy which many people can't grasp.

Currently, the pandemic has limited live musical performance and social gatherings so I've used this time to help fulfill a lifelong dream of putting together a collection of songs that are both personal compositions along with meaningful arrangements of songs by other artists, and hopefully these easy listening selections will become a favorite for all to enjoy including young up-and-coming musicians.

Every August during my early teens, my family and I would attend the St. James Armenian Church's annual "Blessing of the Grapes" ceremony and picnic. As soon we pulled into a parking spot, we could hear the Armenian music of the Roger Krikorian Ensemble and smell the familiar aroma of shish kebab cooking on massive grills. I remember leaping out of the car and making a beeline for the SRO front-row spots directly in front of the bandstand so that I could see my cousin Ken Kalajian up close on guitar! He made playing my favorite instrument look so easy. Always calm with a radiant smile, he made such beautiful music at so many events that celebrated our Armenian heritage.

SEAN SCHULICH

When I play music through my flute, every listener hears their own distinctive story unfold. A shared uniqueness. How wonderful is that? Music is the collective bridge.

—Sean Schulich

I met Sean many years ago when we were both working at a financial services firm in New York City. We are both Tufts University alumni which we learned in our first conversation together. I found Sean to be a fascinating storyteller and loved listening to him speak. When he told me he played the flute, I couldn't wait to get home from work and check out his YouTube videos. Sean pushes the boundaries of the flute in the most soulful, captivating way and his passion for his instrument clearly shows with every move he makes.

ANNAMARIE ZMOLEK

grew up singing all the time with my big Mormon family. My mother loved to get us singing hymns or Christmas carols together, often while trapped in the car and much to the annoyance of some. Both my parents played piano and loved to sing, so music was always around. I was lucky to be on the younger side of the nine siblings.

My older sisters took voice lessons to get better parts in their high school musicals. I would sometimes sit in and thus I got to know Leigh MacClay, a wonderful Denver area teacher. I was a precocious and annoying little kid, but she saw enough talent in me that she agreed to start me in lessons at age 11. I would tape record all my lessons and re-do them every day, so I was able to learn lots of music and make lots of progress through my teen years. I will always be grateful to Leigh for putting so much energy into me, for introducing me to classical music, and eventually helping me get into the Eastman School of Music for my undergrad degree. She started me off with Jazz standards, Broadway, and Folk songs, but eventually snuck in that opera and got me hooked. She gave me

tickets to see my first live opera, which blew my mind. She is an amazing person and educator, and still teaching a bit to this day.

The highest highs of music making are hard to describe without platitudes. As a singer, your body is your instrument, and it can be easy to get lost in nagging thoughts or phlegm or self-obsession.

But every now and again, maybe once or twice a year, time stands still, you feel outside yourself yet completely alive in your own body, and the sound pours out freely and beautifully. Sometimes these moments happen in a rehearsal and the actual performance only carries their echo. Sometimes it is singing in the shower or a particularly resonant parking lot. It can happen onstage in an opera, where you connect deeply to the emotions of a character. You weep as them, you love as them, you might even die as them. It is spine tingling and hair raising and absolutely electric.

I think the frustration in music is that these moments are too rare, and if you reach for them too hard, they elude you further. It also happens that sometimes you have fellow singers who bring out your best, whose voices ring wonderfully with yours. Sadly, they are not always going to be your most frequent collaborators. So, if I know I get to sing with someone who brings out the best in me, I am overjoyed and relish it. I know there may well be long seasons where we don't work together, so I try to fill up the cup while I can.

I don't know what I would tell aspiring musicians. My husband, a fellow singer, would say to get out while you can and get a useful degree. I don't think I would want them to know the ugly side of things. It doesn't do any good to know about that stuff. At the same time, I don't want to fill my students with lies and false hope. I mostly just want young students to get to know all the best music, to fall in love with it like I did, and to make music from the heart as best they can.

I met Annamarie Zmolek in 2018 when she taught voice and piano at LB Music School. She is an outstanding teacher who has motivated many students to make wonderful music. One of my fondest memories of Annamarie was hearing her sing "live" for the first time. I was administrator at the music school at the time and while at the front desk, I suddenly heard her beautiful soprano voice emanating from her studio down the hall as she practiced one of her songs before the school opened. It was a glorious, operatic moment!

BARBARA LIPTON

started playing the flute when I was in the 7th grade. I don't remember why I chose the flute, but once I began to play...I realized that even at the young age of 12, I had found the emotional outlet for myself and my creativity that I hadn't known I needed. I took weekly lessons and every day after school I locked myself in my bedroom and practiced for hours. By the time I was 17 and a senior in high school, I was an outstanding player. Jean Pierre Rampal and James Galway were my idols.

Playing music spoke in ways that even today, I struggle to put into words. I had a traumatic childhood and music "saved" me from myself and transported me to a world of beauty. Music connected me to my emotions and became the outer expression of my inner thoughts and feelings. What I expressed through music was mine...and no one else's. For me, it was emotional freedom.

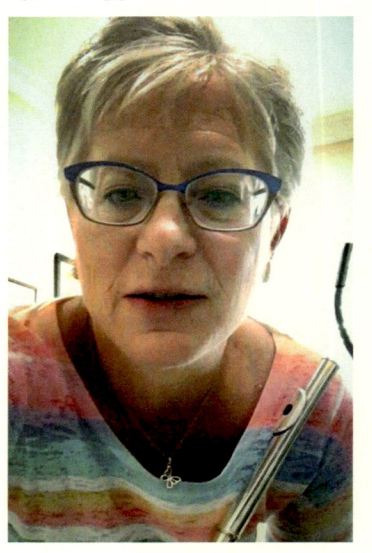

Playing music is truly the window to a person's soul and can evoke powerful emotions in ourselves and others. When we create or listen to music, there are no boundaries to our feelings. Music taught me that emotions are good...feelings are human...and that we all have the common language of music that we can interpret in a way that is personal to us. When we play, we affect others, and that is truly magical. As musicians, we have the power to engage and to move both ourselves and our audience. We must always remember that our music can and will be...transformational.

My friend Barbara and I met in 1981 shortly before promotions in our retail careers brought us from Boston to New York City. We were roommates for several years and I fondly recall the first time she played her flute for me in our apartment. I was mesmerized and moved to (joyful) tears. Knowing how music had been her emotional outlet since she was a young girl, I could clearly see the transformation in her as she played with such passion and intensity.

CHARLOTTE PEARCE

Music was always there, somewhere inside, biding its time in an attempt to find a personal way of releasing its potential for my own satisfaction. Singing was never an option for extracurricular activities at school and I certainly never knew anyone who took voice lessons or was a singer by profession. I was told to play the flute in the school band because it was the easiest to transport on the school bus and would fit in my backpack. At the very least, I was taught to read music, find rhythm and melody—and play alongside others. My short duration in the school band was also the impetus for frustration as I became bored playing music on the flute when I thought how much more gratifying it would be to sing the melody.

For years, singing in the car, the shower, the garage, and the kitchen mostly itched the scratch, though it left me with an ever-growing list of questions about how to sing well. When I was eventually earning my own money and only had myself to look after, I took the leap and signed up for voice lessons. I was impatient to learn the answers to all my questions and eager to improve at lightning speed because I'd waited too long. I also didn't share with many people that I'd signed up for lessons. Somehow, I felt there was a stigma attached to an adult taking voice lessons, like I was trying to be something I wasn't, or that the ship had already sailed and that if I'd wanted to "be someone", the time had passed.

The more I learned, the more I realized how much I didn't know, and the world of music kept unfolding before me, endlessly and intriguingly, leaving my mind buzzing and keeping me awake at night. Even now, with several years of music lessons under my belt, I know that I can't listen to music or watch any music-related videos or content before bed or I will lie awake daydreaming of singing *Les Misérables* on stage, or imagining how it must feel to be Celine Dion or Freddie Mercury, or Andrea Bocelli, people who truly perfected their craft.

Alas, my interests in life now run far and wide but I never leave music behind. It must occasionally take a backseat when the kids are calling the shots, or it's too cold to practice with my local band outside, or when I've paid for ski lessons, school, babysitters and day trips and indulging in a music lesson seems one thing too many.

The two pieces of advice I'd have for any other adult who knows that music can create an engagement in life unlike any other, are these. Be aware and remember how being a part of a musical experience makes you feel. Treasure it, don't neglect it. It's always easy to think that other things should take priority, but you've got to create your own space, whatever that looks like, to participate in music on a regular or even semi-regular basis. It will forever add to who you are as an individual. In addition, having friends who also prioritize music in their lives will help you stay engaged and remember how important it is.

I thought singing was either about getting busted singing in the car at a traffic light or performing for a stadium of fans. I never expected to find the niche treasure that music has brought to my daily life. When I have time, I'll work through songs over and over with people, trying to get the harmonies right, or spend time creating our own versions of songs, or even writing our own. I'm so glad that I was brave enough to give singing a try because it has brought incalculable joy to my life, and I'll never let it go.

I met Charlotte in 2017 at LB Music School where she was studying voice. When I saw her acoustic duo perform at an outdoor concert in 2018, I was so impressed with her vocal talent and how happy she looked while making music. Such a talented singer with important advice to share with other music makers. May she never let that "incalculable joy" go!

NINA DE VITRY

Music is magic. It is an invisible power—one that can guide the emotions in all directions, capture memories, and unify strangers. My greatest joys in music making have been during raw moments of collaboration—when all egos fly out the window, and everyone involved feels supported, comfortable, and free to be their most honest and creative selves. It is a palpable energy. When this happens, the music takes on a life of its own, breathing and dancing. The more I play music, I realize that these are the moments I aspire to. How can I be part of music in a way that does not judge, listens deeply, and supports the whole? I am in love with this endless process of learning and growing. I would encourage aspiring musicians to ask themselves, "When do I feel most excited, inspired, and comfortable in music? What are the instruments, who are the people, or what are the situations that help me to feel this way?"

Follow that, and don't look back.

Nina de Vitry is a jazz-folk multi-instrumentalist, singer, and songwriter. I met Nina in early 2020 at LB Music School when she was living in Boston and available for short-term violin and piano teaching assignments. Her first full-length album "What You Feel Is Real" is a beautiful work of musical artistry. I have such admiration for Nina and am so grateful for the inspiring words of wisdom she shares here.

SAMUEL MOSCOSO

PHOTO CREDIT: MOLLY POSEY ROSSITER

G rowing up, I never really thought I could make music for a living. I dreamed of being a performer and a recording artist, sure. But music as an actual, viable career? I don't think I truly believed it was possible. Which is odd when I think about it, considering I am the son of two professional opera singers. Not one, but both of my parents are artists. Why couldn't I see an artistic path for myself?

Perhaps, subconsciously, I recognized the sacrifice it takes to be an artist. That most of the time you are in a perpetual state of looking for employment or that it often seems like you are waiting on someone else to give you permission to have a career. That even with extensive training and education, quite regularly your work will not be valued and not understood. That audiences go home and the void left behind can be excruciatingly and cripplingly lonely. That your relationships suffer for the sake of your art. That your schedule will be atypical and while you are working, it seems everyone else isn't, so you will watch your loved ones go out to restaurants, and go away on vacations, and build friendships and memories while you are just grateful to work… or while you keep yourself available, *hoping* to work. Yet again, you will find yourself alone. You will watch life happen without you. Or you will be fortunate enough to book a gig that takes you away for months at a time, completely immersed in your art, only to return to find that life happened without you.

Perhaps that is why I did not pursue music for a career. I listened to the world telling me I had to choose a life that was stable and traditional and safe. I did not have to give up music; I simply had to have a more ostensibly sustainable plan that could then allow music to live on the side.

Though it does seem, as it would turn out, music did indeed pursue me.

As much as I sought alternative avenues and traversed other professional paths, music was steadfast, my constant companion, beckoning me to listen;

to breathe; to sing; to create; to come alive!

A supremely accomplished musician friend of mine once said, "I did not set out for music to be my career. I was only going to make music until I figured out what else to do with my life. I just never figured out anything else."

Music is woven into the fabric of who I am. It celebrates with me in achievement, and it grieves with me in loss. It dances with me in my joy, and it encourages me in my doubts. It comforts me in loneliness. It affirms me in my insecurities. It reminds me of my blessings, of those whom I love, and that life is worth living.

Because even in the sacrifice, there is joy. Despite the sting of vulnerability, there is exhilaration! In the face of loneliness, there is authenticity. Even in the midst of uncertainty, there is purpose. In the act of sharing and experiencing and communicating through music, there is humanity. And in moments of incredible and profound privilege, you might see your way through all of the fear and doubt and rejection and grief and sacrifice and find that you were able to create something truly meaningful.

Perhaps music did not pursue me at all. Perhaps, more accurately, it was music that led me in my pursuit of purpose and meaning in the world. Music does not live on the side. It grounds me and centers me. It is the oxygen of my soul, the language in which I communicate with the world around me and how I understand what the world wishes to teach. Without it, I am rendered speechless, both for lack of something to say as well as the breath with which to say it. How could I make any other choice but to follow its lead?

Actor, singer, composer and self-described dreamer Samuel Moscoso had me at his sparkling "Hello" the moment he entered the lobby of LB Music School many years ago to teach voice and piano lessons to several students whose teacher was out ill that day. Samuel's musical knowledge, talent and passion for sharing it was a winning combination that day I met him and, as I was to learn, every day of his life. Born in Germany to operatic parents Emilio and Deborah Moscoso, Samuel has performed at the White House, for Pope John Paul II at the Vatican, and as a featured artist on stages across the U.S. and Europe. He also regularly performs throughout the Northeast with the KTO Band.

DANA WELTS

Having music in your life is like having a best friend who is always available. You may lose touch for a time or have disagreements but when you reconnect it's like the distance never occurred. Your relationship with your instrument(s), unlike your relationships with your friends or your day job scene, is perfectly equitable—you always get back exactly what you put into it. If you neglect it, you lose some skills. If you practice (I mean really practice and give yourself new challenges, not just play what you already know), you improve. No exceptions here- perfectly predictable and under your control. Finally, playing alone can be consoling and rewarding but playing with others expands the magic by several orders of magnitude. There is nothing—no relationship, no team, no school cohort, no office department, no nothing that compares with being in a band. If you've never been in a band this may be impossible to understand. If you've been in bands, you already know this.

My high school friend Dana started his lifelong love affair with music in the third grade playing in a small family combo. He joined his first rock band at age 15 and began writing songs in his early twenties. Dana played professionally until he was 40 years old when he took a hiatus from performing (to generate some "real money" for the family). He resumed gigging at age 60 and is a guitar player and backup singer in several diverse (country, doo wop, rock and classic rock) bands, playing 90-100 shows per year since 2012.

KEVIN O'SHAUGHNESSY

I f you want to get an idea of what it's like to learn just about anything, let alone an instrument, watch a child learn to walk. First, it takes them a while to develop the muscles to sit up. Then they have to stand. And they fall down...a lot!

They use furniture or help from their parents to take their first steps. And they fall down some more. The child may cry when they fall down but they smile again when they get back up. It takes them about four to six months before they're walking and running under their own power.

They'll practice walking and running and, over the next several months, they'll get really good at it. Then they might decide that they want to try jumping, and the whole process of trying and falling and trying and falling starts all over again.

People tend to use the expression, "It's a marathon, not a sprint" to describe anything that requires patience and a slow, steady pace. I hear this a lot to describe learning an instrument as well and I think it's the *wrong* analogy. Why? Because both marathons and sprints eventually end.

So let's look at how they end. First, both marathons and sprints have fixed distances to be run. Second, they're both races, meaning that someone needs to win. In other words, once the distance has been surpassed, the race is over and whoever completed the race first is the winner. This is not the case when learning an instrument.

I think the better analogy is that learning an instrument is a growth cycle. Every living thing starts from some kind of seed, moves through a period of growth, and eventually becomes about as big as it's going to get but it keeps growing until it eventually dies. The initial growth period is the hardest but the advancements are the most obvious. Later growth periods are easier, but the advancements are less obvious.

Take learning the guitar. When you learn your first chords and your first songs, your improvement is obvious and appears to move forward

in leaps and bounds. This makes sense when you consider that you started from nothing so every new skill is going to have a big impact.

Once you've built a repertoire of songs and you've gotten comfortable with the basic techniques, attention is generally moved to more advanced techniques. These could be things like articulation and dynamics. These are things that add musicality to your performance but are not always the most obvious. For example, playing without vibrato is far less obvious than playing a wrong chord.

What happens after you've learned basic and advanced techniques? Have you "won" guitar? Of course not. Hopefully, you continue to play and deepen your enjoyment of playing while also deepening your understanding of the techniques you've learned. In other words, you keep growing. The only way this cycle ends is if you decide for whatever reason to stop playing.

I met Kevin at LB Music School in 2017 where he was teaching guitar and piano and I was administrator. If he had a break between lessons, he'd come up front and within minutes, I would be treated to a conversation in which he would so generously share his knowledge about different aspects of music-making. A talented singer/songwriter and guitarist, Kevin has played in hundreds of shows, created scores for film, documentaries and theater and performed on hundreds of songs for aspiring music-makers. In 2015, Kevin produced his debut solo album solo album Persistence of Vision.

DEBORAH MOSCOSO

Music has been such an intricate part of my life, it's hard to separate it or think of it as just something I do. Music has taught me so much. I came to have it as a career in a seemingly erratic or offhand manner. My professional roles in two opera companies opened up by happenstance. My first contract came because they wanted to keep my husband; the second because I thought I had to at least pretend to look for a job in order to collect unemployment and ended up getting more than I thought possible. I never thought as a young person that this would be my life. In some ways I even fought against it, leaving singing for a whole year after I returned from singing in an opera company chorus. But music would not let me go and kept insisting that I return and pay attention.

Music is ministry and fulfillment, solace and respite. It has been there through all these amazing, scary, critical and heart-wrenching times. Making music was solace when my mother lay dying. Music was my work and purpose when my sisters died; making music and earning my degree instilled great pride in my father; making music was a respite when my husband was diagnosed with a deadly disease and I didn't know if he would live or die and leave me with two small children.

Music has influenced my whole life. The way I was taught singing has been a gift. I was taught to sing, deliberately, focusing on how the body works, listening to and feeling how the sound is produced; noticing how

the breath leads everything. The work on breath translates into everyday breathing; the focus I bring to singing translates to how I go about my day; what is important here; keep breathing, be steady, notice how everything hangs together and influences everything else.

Music is not only about production but also about life. The characters I have met in its poetry and drama, especially the women but also the men, have shown me what true love is, what betrayal looks like, what weakness is and what it destroys. It has taught me how to meet life: keep going no matter what you meet. It has taught me persistence and shown me courage, an attribute I strive over and over to possess.

I am so grateful.

In 2017, I met Deborah at LB Music School where she is an outstanding voice and piano teacher. When I was administrator at the school, I enjoyed our many conversations about music-making. I was fascinated by the stories she shared about the years (1972 -1980) when she and her beloved husband Emilio lived in Germany where they were opera singers at various opera companies. Deborah is also an adult choir director where she shares her passion for singing and teaching with her devoted choir members. Last but not least, she is the mother of Samuel Moscoso who is another wonderful music maker in my life.

LISA GIANNETTI

Your very best self-expression is to honor who you are. If your passion is in music (or really anything!), explore it to the fullest. And remember, any self-doubt is just noise: drown it out with music!

—Lisa Giannetti

I met Lisa in 2017 at LB Music School where she was a voice student and a member of the A Capella Group. I remember the first time I heard Lisa sing. It was at an Open Mic event many years ago at the music school. I was struck by the strength and range of her voice and knew she was destined for vocal greatness. Lisa has performed locally as a duo with her guitar accompanist. One of my favorites is her soul-searing rendition of Dolly Parton's "Jolene".

LORRIE DEKAY

s there anyone who grew up in the 60s who did NOT want to be in a band at some point? What good fortune to be part of that generation, following the Big Band era, early days of rock and roll, into the British Invasion, folk music and protest songs...we had it all. I can't remember a time when music wasn't a part of my life. As the eldest in a family of 7 kids, there was no money for music lessons, but that does not mean we didn't have music education, thanks to Dad.

My dad, a printer by trade, was a Renaissance Man. He loved music, art, and all things Italian. He was an accomplished guitar player and taught my sister and me the words to all his best songs, classics from the 40s. I still know the words to this day. On the weekends, Dad played record albums for us, from children's music like Prokofiev's Peter and The Wolf, which taught us the different instruments in the process, to music with a story like Grieg's Peer Gynt Suites or Mussorgsky's Pictures at an Exhibition. He loved opera and took me to my first (Carmen) at the Boston Opera House. A huge fan of Gilbert and Sullivan's operettas, he made sure we were all well versed in those as well. For good measure, we also got a good dose of his personal favorite, Belgian jazz guitarist Django Reinhardt, and Marian McPartland's jazz piano. We watched Leonard Bernstein's Young People's Concerts with the NY Philharmonic, and Mitch Miller's sing along. There were several albums of Alan Sherman's parody songs in the record rack, as well as a Time Life series with classic American folk music (the transportation album was

a favorite with Casey Jones, The Erie Canal, and John Henry). To this day, I credit my dad with instilling a love of music into my soul. All kinds of music.

There were years of singing in church choir, junior high chorus, playing guitar for Folk Mass with a few friends during High School...but not a BAND. I saved up and bought my first guitar in 7th grade. Dad showed me some chords, but he played barre chords which were a little tough for me. Enter my junior high friend Gail Hendry, who shared her talents with a few of her classmates, and we formed a folk club. For whatever reason, the guitar never made it through college with me (too many bio and chem labs, too many parties). My guitar went to a very talented niece (now an elementary school teacher who writes and performs her own music in her off hours). Music was always there for listening but not for playing. There was a brief love affair with banjo in the late 70s, but trying to self-teach with Bela Fleck tapes was not optimal for that to progress. I did become proficient with a kazoo, does that count?

Little did I know I would be 57 years old before I joined a band, playing an instrument that was never on my radar. After 25 years of moving around for my husband's career, including a 6-year stint overseas in Nigeria, he retired and we relocated one last time, to the Pacific Northwest, an hour east of Portland OR in the small town of White Salmon, WA. For fun, I took an adult education class for ukulele. A quick Dad note: Dad was also an excellent uke player. For his 80th birthday, my sisters and I bought ukes, and I taught them how to play Happy Birthday so we could serenade him as he had done for us every year on our birthdays. No matter how far flung, we'd get a call with a song. I had not progressed past Happy Birthday, so Uke Class was a great incentive. I thought I'd be the only one showing up for the class, but there was a roomful! It was fun, I learned more songs, played with others, and learned about transposing to different keys. So you think I joined the Gorge Ukelele Orchestra, right? Wrong.

During the course of the Uke lessons, I came upon another band playing at a local festival. What joyful music; I had to find out more about this Jamba Marimba Band! I later met one of the members, who decided I should come along to practice some night to see what it was all about. That night, they taught me 2 chords to play along with "Wimoweh", and I was hooked. They were looking for new people, preferably with some skills, but I promised to learn as quickly as possible. Our marimbas are C scale, how hard can that be? I took a few lessons from one of the most accomplished players, spent hours in my basement that winter learning parts on a borrowed marimba with my mp3 player loaded with band songs, a test of my husband's patience and ear drums. By the next performance season, in the summer of 2008, I had parts in many of the songs. The early years of singing in chorus paid off with an ear that was adept at hearing the parts, and how they worked together.

Marimba bands are really big in the PNW. We have an opportunity to hear the best, and take workshops, at the annual Zimfest with musicians from Zimbabwe. Jamba Marimba is currently an all women band of 9, ranging in age from the 50s to 93. The eldest, Irene, is a violin/viola teacher who learned to play marimba at 70 and we play in her garage/driveway. There are a bass, baritone, 2 tenor and 3 soprano marimbas in our stable, along with a few djembes and hoshos for added percussion. Favorite gigs are local farmer's markets in the summer, winery patios, park fundraisers and private parties. Songs are mostly from Zimbabwe, but we also play more recognizable tunes like "Jamaica Farewell", "La Bamba", and "In The Mood". One of our members arranged "Blue Moon" for a private Blue Moon party that has become a regular on the gig list. And the year many of us turned 64, we played that one, too!

Wednesday practice sessions with my girlfriends have been a highlight of my week for more than 10 years. Even days when I don't feel like going, once we start playing, energy returns. There have been challenging times. You can't have 9 or so women in a group without some kind of drama, but the bumps have been infrequent. The biggest challenge has been the pandemic. Covid has disrupted our sisterhood, and left a huge gap in our lives. We are hoping to reconvene with better weather and vaccines all around. In the meantime, I've signed up for online hand drumming classes, because learning new stuff is so good for your brain, and that djembe class I took at Zimfest in 2019 seems a distant memory.

It's never too late to learn something new, and making music takes life to a new level.

I met Lorrie in high school and, though we were not in a lot of the same classes, we were in the same homeroom for several years which gave me the opportunity to enjoy her quick wit and wonderful sense of humor nearly every weekday morning.

I love what Lorrie shares here about the musical education her beloved and very cool Dad provided to her and her siblings at a very young age. I already knew that she did finally end up in a...BAND because I saw a video of her playing in Jamba Marimba on Facebook one day several years ago. And thanks to this wonderful story, I now know the steps of her musical journey that led to achieving that goal!

CHRIS BECKER

While I do enjoy composing alone in my studio—notating musical ideas onto score paper or creating ambient or beat-driven soundscapes in Ableton Live and playing back the results for an audience of one (me)—collaborating with artists who aren't musicians including choreographers, filmmakers, and visual artists, has inspired some of my best work. But before such a collaboration begins, I make it clear I'm not a human jukebox; that what I'm going to bring to the project is me, unfiltered, although I'm willing to shape and revise my contributions to the work. Thankfully, the artists I collaborate with, such as multi-disciplinary artist Jil Guyon, who creates videos that blur the lines between performance art, film noir and painterly abstraction, want that unique "thing" that distinguishes my music from a zip file of samples. I believe artists should be uncompromising in their vision and yet generous and humble enough to work as collaborators in order to create something truly new and perhaps change the way people listen and see.

Why hire yourself out as a copycat? As Oscar Wilde said, "Be yourself; everyone else is already taken."

My virtual friendship with writer, editor and composer Chris Becker began in 2015 when he announced the publication of his critically acclaimed "Freedom of Expression: Interviews With Women in Jazz". It's a superb collection of in-depth interviews with 37 female jazz musicians of all ages, nationalities, and races, who represent nearly every style of jazz one can imagine. I've bought many copies of this book to give as gifts and it never disappoints. As a composer, Chris has created music for dance, experimental video, and mixed-media installations. I have remained connected with Chris via social media since 2015 and try to keep up with all of his brilliant writing and creative projects.

CHRISTINA KENT-JETHA

**What do you consider to be the most important ideas
and concepts to impart to aspiring musicians?**

Everyone belongs in the world of music. We all have a unique voice whether it is expressed through singing, guitar, drums, piano or tuba. Music is a space where our stories, emotions and unique experiences can be poignantly expressed.

Sadly, I think many people feel like they don't have permission to be a part of this beautiful art form. They get scared away from music because they think they need to be perfect or sound exactly like their favourite musician.

Music does not need perfection.

Music needs authenticity and honesty.

So whether your voice is smooth, robust, feathery or rough; it belongs exactly as it is (imagine if Louis Armstrong decided his voice was too rough?! What a loss that would have been for the musical landscape!).

Music moves us most when it is honest, heartfelt expression. So make your number one priority being yourself and expressing yourself sincerely through your instrument, because your voice is essential.

Treasure your love of music and hold it close to your heart. Continually come back to your "why" for pursuing music. Perhaps you do it because it makes you smile or because it helps you to express yourself in a way that nothing else can. Maybe it makes you feel connected to yourself and others, challenges you in a nourishing way or makes you feel alive. Whatever your reason, anchor yourself in your "why" and let it nourish you as you experience the beautiful, lifelong journey.

I met Christina in 2019 at LB Music School where she taught voice and piano. In 2021, she founded the Mindful Sound Studio, an in-person and online music education space that emphasizes a holistic approach to vocal development. Christina's in-depth knowledge, her vibrant spirit and her passion for helping her students discover their own unique connection to their voice have helped so many aspiring music makers of all ages develop into creative and expressive singers.

JOHNNY BLOOD

Music is our original language, international language, and probably will be our interstellar language as well. Embrace it with all your love and conviction, it won't let you down. If you are considering making a living as a musician, be well advised to have a secondary source of income. During the Pandemic of 2020 many musicians were stripped of their livelihoods for safety protocols. Some may disagree, but I believe we are essential workers! I look forward to performing for everyone again as soon as safety permits. Keep a song in your heart every day!

Johnny Blood is a guitarist, composer and producer based in East Hampton, NY. I met Johnny when I lived in Bridgehampton in the late 1990s and had the good fortune of taking guitar lessons with him in my home. I also frequently enjoyed seeing Johnny play live with The Nancy Atlas Project at local venues on the East End. I was the one dancing as close to the band as possible so I could watch Johnny create musical magic while his fretting fingers traveled up and down his guitar neck at lightning speed.

JOSEPH BENZOLA

An artist's main duty is to create work of integrity and beauty in their personal form. You can try to create with others in mind but these pieces rarely succeed because the wrong intent is present. If you do not truly believe in what you are doing, you will never truly satisfy your soul.

—Joseph Benzola

My album of improvisations started off as a one-off experiment, then morphed into a weekly investigation of my solo language via improvisation. Like all creative individuals, you eventually reach a crossroads with periods of severe self-doubt and self-worth. I've never had the opportunity to present my music to an audience on any consistent basis. My recorded body of work has been documented in one form or another since the early 1990's. Though well received by a few, it still is cloaked in invisibility due to many reasons.

So what to do??? I decided to take the matter in my own hands. I decided to document my "Live Performances" via my iPhone and Zoom iOS mic and post these improvisations on FB and Vimeo. Yes, I know.... not a novel idea but it did provide a solution. Though I have fought the impulse from time to time and deleted my recordings with military precision from the public record, I STILL have this need to create music and to share it with

an audience—whether that audience is in the flesh or a collection of "0's" and "1's" via the internet.

I approached each "performance" as if I were in front of a live audience. I think that this mindset was of the utmost importance as it helped push me to go to the next level to communicate to this live virtual audience. And like a live performance, there was no going back to redo... they are for keeps—mistakes and all!!!

The performances were recorded live in my studio. They investigate concepts that I have been working on for a number of years. What this process proved to me is that I would be able to communicate and perform these ideas solo without the input of other musicians.

To quote Robert Fripp, I became "a small, intelligent, highly mobile unit." The performances range from solo piano and drums to combinations of acoustic and electronic instrumentation. I have tried to come up with an individual language, vocabulary, and sound based on my multitude of influences from jazz, classical, world, and electronic music.

· ·

Joseph Benzola is an independent multi-instrumentalist, composer and producer living in New York. My virtual friendship with Joseph began in 2016. I would look forward to his weekly posts of his solo "Live Performances" improvs on percussion or piano. I am also grateful to Joseph for his role in my own music discovery of a wide spectrum of music makers thanks to his daily "Now Playing" posts. I can't wait to see the next album cover strategically poised in front of his turntable and the blue lights of his McIntosh amp. Sometimes, a glass of wine or a cup of coffee is in the picture to complete the mood. If I am not familiar with the artist or the album, it goes on my TO LISTEN TO LIST that I keep on the side of my desk. Thanks to Joseph's impeccable taste, I am never disappointed.

· ·

ETHAN DEPUY

Music is all about communication. Decide what you want to say, then say it LOUDLY.

—Ethan Depuy

I met Ethan in 2017 at LB Music School. He was teaching voice and piano to children and adults. I always admired his brilliance, teaching style and, of course, his outstanding vocal and piano artistry—and how he was able to make a connection with every student regardless of their skill level, anxiety level or their mood on lesson day. Ethan is a talented, well-respected tenor in the world of opera as well as a member of the prestigious Handel and Haydn Society and Boston Baroque professional choruses.

JOSÉE POIRIER

Belonging

When my voice instructor had gently but firmly encouraged me to check out the a capella group she led, my immediate reaction was to doubt that I would fit in or that I could be a voice that enriched the ensemble. It was also a self-preserving reaction in the sense that I did not want to share my singing time: it was my *me* time and an activity I had never done publicly. The thought of singing amongst others who likely sang better and knew more about MUSIC terrified me. I feared it would take away from the pleasure of singing by making me think about it as an act of performance, where I would be judged and required to work to meet others' expectations. Music was the area in my life that was centered on being and feeling, not on performing and I felt very protective of that.

I finally caved in out of curiosity and anticipated delight in hearing a capella singing. My worst-case scenarios did not concretize: the group was so kind and generous that I felt included from the get-go. I rapidly learned a lot about music theory and singing. It was a safe environment where people came to have fun making music. Where people tried to get it right to honour the song, not because of peer pressure. Where mistakes were made and were part of the musical adventure. It was a friendly space where singers enjoyed themselves and forged new friendships.

Yet that's not what surprised me the most about joining an a cappella group. It was how intimate singing with others is. By singing together we co-create, we uplift one another, we celebrate everyone's voice. Joining voices is connecting into an immediate closeness from which emerges a beautiful vulnerability and strength. Even when a voice part sounds somewhat dull or unremarkable in isolation, it transcends into a sophisticated ensemble when all voices are combined. And then you realize, feeling it in your soul, how your voice was needed to render the exquisite result. You also realize that, as in life, we all have a part to play—sometimes one that is more supportive and sometimes one that is more of a guiding force. And in the end, you are forced to admit that you *can* make a contribution—that the whole isn't quite as rich without every voice, including your voice. Because your voice matters. And you're amazed to find a deep life lesson where you initially didn't think you belonged.

Finding one's voice.

It took me decades. Years of singing in the shower, in the car, in the house, when no one's around. Years to admit to myself or understand that singing was something that moved me in a way nothing else did. Then one day, I took the leap and called a nearby music school for voice lessons. "Nothing to lose" I thought. "If I'm awful at it at least I'll learn *something* and I can stop after a few lessons."

My voice instructor, perhaps unsurprisingly, was more supportive of my efforts. She repeated that talent wasn't the key but rather that practice was. She insisted that my "beautiful voice" only needed to be set free. She suggested that I develop my singing through songs I liked and explore my personal style. So we chose songs to work on together and she gave me exercises to develop my technical skill. Months into my lessons I was learning a great deal and doing things with my voice I had never thought I could do. Still, I didn't believe her when she said I sang beautifully (and I continue to struggle believing her!). I think she'd say that *she* knows something *I'm* just not seeing (or hearing) yet.

As time went by my instructor kept gently pushing me out of my comfort zone. One day I'd push through; the next time I'd fall back. I began realizing the psychological component to learning how to sing. My intellect understood what she explained; my ear heard the high note. I would then open my mouth and...nothing would come out. Or I'd move forward an inch closer to what I was aiming to do for the first time and would fail at the last step before reaching it. Sometimes it was a matter of trying repeatedly until I achieved it. But often, it wasn't that my voice *couldn't* do it: it was that I would not *let* it. Just like the first time at the gym when I ran a mile at my personal record or jumped a box higher than a foot, my body was ready to meet the challenge, but my head was too afraid to let it try.

I have learned that singing is a deeply personal act. Your instrument is literally yourself and you can feel very exposed by it. It's also the best way for me to connect with my emotions. Singing makes me feel more whole. It's a channel for self-realization. It unlocks a fuller range of human experiences. It has also been a tool for me to confront the times when I don't feel safe or good enough to occupy space and be heard.

To believe I can do it, I can be it. And not get in my own way.

I met Josée at LB Music School several years ago when she studied voice and also performed in Katie O'Brien's a cappella group while living and working in Boston. One of my fondest memories of Josée is her 2019 recital performance of "Je T'oublierai" by Isabelle Boulay. When she was introduced on stage, she first spoke in English about the background and lyrics of this emotional song before singing it in French. This created an immediate connection between the singer and her audience which was wonderful to see. They not only heard Josée's melodic French vocals; they understood what the song was about. I admire Josée for sharing her personal musical journey with us and for being so open about how she found "her voice".

CAROLINE DOCTOROW

To someone who has chosen to be a professional musician I would say—don't let any one person stop you! For instance, if your bass player quits with very short notice, don't cancel your shows or wait to book new dates as you search for a replacement. Keep forging ahead on all levels, making sure that you can perform as a solo artist if need be. At your core, be a self-contained and self-reliant entertainer, performing as many of your songs as you can. The rest is icing on the cake.

I met my friend and singer-songwriter Caroline in 1995 about a year after moving from Manhattan to Bridgehampton NY. I studied guitar with her until my business travel schedule back then made it impossible to stick with weekly lessons. I enjoyed seeing Caroline perform live with her band at many local venues and it didn't take long for our friendship to form. Often referred to as a great champion of American folk music, Caroline has released a total of eleven solo albums all of which can still be heard on folk and Americana stations worldwide. She is the daughter of the late world-renowned author E.L. Doctorow. Even though we haven't seen each other in a long time, we have kept in touch over the years.

LEON JANIKIAN

I grew up in the center of what was a large concentration of Armenian immigrants. All of my aunts and uncles and my four grandparents were born in Marash during the Ottoman period. My parents, however, were both born in the U.S. which is why my paternal grandfather gave me the nickname "Yankee Boy"... his only grandson born to parents born here.

As a kid growing up, I would often hear the music that my family listened to when they had a group gathering, a fairly frequent event. Often these gatherings would include the whole family singing songs they recalled from their youth in the "Old Country". I wasn't aware of it then, but I listened carefully...more carefully than I realized until I started saxophone lessons in seventh grade. My hope was that I would be good enough to play in a band. Never was I focused on making music a career choice.

At that time, it was common for families to travel to Camp Ararat in Maynard MA. There we would enjoy great food, camaraderie, and music. Music performed, usually, by a trio of musicians who captured my ear and created in me a lifelong love for our folkloric music. I was always glued to the bandstand watching and listening, mesmerized by the music and by the skill of the performers. I can recall hearing Oudi Hrant, Louis Matalon, George Elbag, Harry Hasekian, Marko Melkon and "Oil Man Charlie" Jerahian among many others.

At home I would play the songs I heard on my saxophone but I wasn't the only one. Many young men were also playing instruments and learning the music. It wasn't long before we had a cadre of young Armenian boys playing music from the Old Country for our pleasure and for the fun we all had together.

After about a year on the saxophone I switched to the clarinet. I became an obsessed player often practicing for hours. My repertoire became orchestral music, concerti, some Jazz, and, of course, Armenian folkloric music. I still recall the first "event" I ever played in public. In the church hall at St. James, my friends and I played for a youth group social event. The die was cast...I would be a musician.

I studied music at various music schools, earned my academic credentials and had a career in academia for many years. During that time I played at thousands of "kef" events, cabarets, restaurants, hundreds of weddings.

I am still doing it today. By my count I have played for 62 years. As an Armenian musician I have traveled fairly extensively and had many wonderful experiences. Most of all, I have played music with a wonderful group of professional musicians. We have great respect for each other. I have been very fortunate in my musical life...thanks to Camp Ararat, Uncle Aram's house, and all those exemplar musicians that pushed all my buttons.

For most of my childhood and teen years, I associated only one person with the clarinet—and that was Leon. Whether a family wedding, church picnic or any Armenian social event, Leon and his memorable clarinet solos were prominently featured in the band. You could find me "glued to the bandstand" at our church picnics watching this brilliant musician bring Armenian folkloric music to life. As Associate Professor Emeritus in Music at Northeastern University, Leon has inspired many music makers over the years, helping them to achieve their goals, and he is still making music today.

JENN BOBZIN

The middle of any process is, quite honestly, *messy*. Partway through a home haircut? Your poor brother has a mushroom head. Learning how to drive stick? You stall, even after you think you've gotten the hang of it. The process of learning any musical skill is no different! *Everybody* inevitably makes music that sounds bad (and sometimes hilarious). Trust that this is part of the process and embrace your wrong notes! Laugh at your goofy accidental improvisations and celebrate even your smallest musical achievements (like *finally* getting that transition right). Eventually, you'll be able to play the music you've always wanted to play and, in the meantime, enjoy your musical journey—mistakes and all.

I met Jenn in 2019 at LB Music School where she teaches voice, piano and ukulele. She is an outstanding music maker and instructor. Whether she's introducing the basics of music to a 4 year old or advanced vocal techniques to an adult, Jenn continues to inspire all of her students to enjoy their musical journey "mistakes and all". Her favorite part of teaching is seeing the look of pure joy on her students' faces as they achieve their musical goals. I love Jenn's voice…especially when she performs her beautiful renditions of Regina Spektor's songs.

JEFF TAMARKIN

A Rock 'n' Roll Dream Deferred—On Un-Becoming a Musician

There's nothing more heartwarming than a follow-your-dream story. My own dream took shape when I was 11 years old. Like millions of other kids in America and around the world, I saw The Beatles on *The Ed Sullivan Show* and I knew instantly what I was going to do with my life: I, too, was going to be a rock star.

It all seemed so easy. You chose an instrument, found some kindred souls, formed a band, made a record, and hit the top of the charts. The next thing you knew, screaming girls were clawing at you, your picture was on the covers of all the teen magazines, your pockets were lined with cash and you never had to work at a real job. What could be better?

I decided to be a great drummer. I'd always enjoyed banging on things so I might as well bang on the drums. I managed to convince my parents to plunk down the money for a shiny new set of blue-sparkle Ludwig drums from the Sam Ash music store in Hempstead, Long Island, set them up in the basement and...Hey, wait a second, this wasn't as easy as it looked.

Playing the drums was difficult, I soon discovered. Your hands and feet didn't always follow your brain's instructions.

Every afternoon, after school, I'd rush home, place a record on my parents' console stereo, crank up the volume and grab my sticks. I loved bashing away, becoming a de facto member of the Beatles and the Stones, the Dave Clark Five (they were led by a drummer!) and the Animals. But as hard as I tried, I never managed to sound as good as the guys on those records.

I needed to take lessons. Mom? Dad? Can I have some more money, please?

A local guy who was in an actual rock band became my first—and, as it turned out, only—drum teacher. I explained to him that I wanted to join a band and become famous. I just needed to learn how to play. He laughed. He'd been playing drums for a few years, and he was unable to get recognition outside of the local circuit, playing parties and dances, the occasional battle of the bands. You see, he told me, there were a lot of other kids with the same goal, and only the very best would make it.

The instructor told me that if I truly wanted to be a drummer, I needed to start with the rudiments. Becoming a rock star would have to wait until I could play properly.

"What's a rudiment?" I inquired.

I took lessons for a year or so, but I was bored. Playing paradiddles and rolls, one after another, endlessly, wasn't fun. Blasting the Gentrys' "Keep on Dancing" and trying to imitate whatever that drummer was doing at the beginning (um, it's called a roll), attempting to pick up the backbeat to Fontella Bass' funky "Rescue Me," that was fun!

I kept at it, eventually finding some fellow middle school guys who also played. We formed a band called the Strokes of Tyme, the hip spelling an homage of sorts to the other great misspelled bands of the era: Beatles, Byrds, etc. (Led Zeppelin wasn't around yet.)

We sucked. We really, really sucked.

Nonetheless, I was having a great time, and as rock music evolved, my basement exercises evolved along with it. Now I was playing along to the Doors, Jefferson Airplane, the Who, Jimi Hendrix! A handful of good friends and I formed a new band. This one was called the Freewheelin' Ultimato, taking its odd, era-appropriate moniker from random, spoken lines in two old-time TV shows we found hilarious for some long-forgotten reason.

This band was, to be sure, much better than the Strokes of Tyme. By that time, I could do a few things on the drums, or at least maintain a basic beat, and some of the band members could actually play—a little. Some couldn't play at all, but hey, we loved getting together and trying our best to make a song sound like it was supposed to.

We rocked out on hits of the day and some cool underground faves by bands like the Chambers Brothers and the Blues Project. We were sorta punk progenitors too, in our own weird way: We actually landed a few gigs, playing Sweet 16 parties, and ended our sets with a wild medley of early rock 'n' roll classics by Jerry Lee Lewis and Little Richard, incorporating a bit of theatricality by tossing bags of confetti into the crowd and kicking over the drums the way the Who's Keith Moon did (we didn't know at the time that he had a sponsor who supplied him with new ones for free if he broke something.)

There were no screams for us, but even a half-hearted "You guys sounded pretty good," coming from a pretty girl, made it all worthwhile.

That quintet—which sometimes rehearsed in the garage of my parents' home, making us a bona fide garage band (sometimes neighbors even came over to complain about the racket)—didn't last long either, so it was back to jamming along to records for me, occasionally getting a jam session going with other locals who could pluck out a few tunes. (Some of them went on to become actual professional musicians.)

By the early '70s though, the times they were a-changin' for me. I'd decided to move to the Bay Area, which meant leaving the drums behind. With my car loaded to the brim with our belongings, a friend and I headed west, found a cheap apartment, menial jobs, lots of rock concerts, parties galore...but no drums.

I missed them.

A couple of years into my California stay, I hatched a plan. Some people I knew lived on a sizable plot of land north of San Francisco that had an unused shed in the back. They needed a new roommate. The nearest neighbors were far enough away that they wouldn't be bothered by the pounding. I drove all the way back home to Long Island, put the drums in the backseat of the car, and drove all the way back to California. It felt good to be playing again.

But then it happened: the realization. As I struggled once again to kick out a solo that even vaguely emulated one that had left an arena filled with fans slack-jawed, I put down the sticks and admitted to myself that I was simply never going to be a very good drummer.

While I very much enjoyed playing, and relished the outlet, I had neither the skill nor the ambition to hold down the rhythm in a band that was even 10 percent as good as the ones I listened to every day of my life. It wasn't easy to admit it, but it was true.

Some ten years after I first put sticks to snare, I began to lose interest in playing the drums. But simultaneously, I found another way to express my passion for music. I had always enjoyed writing, and I'd been told by teachers and others that I was pretty good at it. I knew a whole lot about rock music and loved reading the various magazines devoted to the subject: *Rolling Stone, Creem, Rock Scene, Circus, Hit Parader, Crawdaddy*. There was even a local one called *BAM* (Bay Area Music) that did a great job of chronicling the San Francisco scene of the late '70s.

Why not combine that knowledge of music—and my strong opinions on the topic—with the hunger I had nurtured for writing? It's not as if I had anything else going on anyway.

By 1976, I'd decided to finish up college at San Francisco State University

(I'd dropped out of college when I left New York for Cali). While I was a student there, after attending the Band's "Last Waltz" concert at Winterland in 1976, on an impulse I submitted a review to the school's newspaper. It was accepted and I was asked to write more. After a couple of months, they made me the Arts Editor—I had no experience or journalistic training whatsoever, but they didn't seem to mind. A college newspaper editor, not a room full of teenage music lovers, had given me my first real sense of worth in the field of music.

With those credentials in hand, I sent a few clips to *BAM*. I heard back right away: How would I like to interview some local bands?

I had never conducted an interview, and I was nervous as hell the first few times, but I quickly discovered that I felt right at home speaking with musicians about their lives and art. Soon, I was spending a considerable amount of time interviewing successful artists (including members of Jefferson Starship, a band whose members I would later come to know well when I wrote a book about them and their predecessors, Jefferson Airplane) and reviewing concerts and records. I became a regular contributor to *BAM*.

By the end of 1977, aware that the rock scene in New York had become newly vibrant, that something called punk rock was the rage there—I'd already seen Patti Smith, Talking Heads and a few other NYC bands in San Francisco—I thought it might be time to head back to the homeland and see if I could get a regular writing gig going. I packed the car—the drums once again stuffed into the backseat—and turned it around, heading east.

That was 45 years ago. Since then, I've never lacked for work writing about music. I've also served as an editor for numerous print magazines and websites. I've written countless articles and reviews, and interviewed thousands of artists working in nearly every musical genre, moving beyond rock to jazz, world music, blues, folk, country, and more. I've met hundreds of the most talented creative figures of the past half-century in the process.

Becoming a rock star was, for me, a dream deferred. As it turned out, the best thing I could do for the music was to not make any, but rather to share with other fans what I thought they might enjoy listening to, and why.

I never played the drums again—I gave them to my brother, who became a formidable player and has worked with many bands over the course of several decades—but I've worn out more typewriters and computers than I could ever hope to count.

As you can see from this wonderful essay, I certainly lucked out by asking my friend Jeff if he would like to be included in my book. We are so grateful that the brilliant Editor of Best Classic Bands, a website devoted to classic rock, decided to combine his knowledge of music and his hunger for writing so that we could learn more about the music makers in our lives and be introduced to new ones!

Music journalism is at its best in Jeff's hands. I bet he was a better drummer than he admits but we're so happy that he ultimately chose those typewriters and computers as his instruments!

I must make special mention here of Jeff's wife and novelist Caroline Leavitt whom I met 65 years ago in first grade. Had Caroline and I not become buddies, I would never have met Jeff! My first-ever performance in a live band was with Caroline and another classmate Charlene in fifth grade. I played my Uncle Hank's bongos on our original composition "We Ride An Old School Bus". Our band earned a standing ovation from our teacher and classmates in our first (and last!) gig.

CHARLES KALAJIAN

As an educator and performer, the most important element to me is to be mindful that music has healing power. Music feeds our souls, so it's my job to not only play notes on a page but to also add the emotion and energy to both the music I perform and the instruction I give students. Yes, technique and theory are a necessary component, but the unifying language for musicians is the context, i.e. the ability to read notes in tandem with the ability to connect with other musicians. By performing as a unit, we each elevate the energy of others.

This is especially true for me as a percussionist. The rhythm section needs to have a heightened awareness of which groove will enhance the melody. Technique only works with teamwork. Creativity is balanced by discipline and all the elements come together when a musician feels and embraces both the notes on the page and the musicians of the stage.

My cousin Charles is a Percussion Instructor at Rhode Island Philharmonic Orchestra and Music School and a topnotch drummer. There are so many inspiring words of wisdom here. His last sentence could stand alone as the best advice a musician could offer to aspiring music makers who want to play with others. Charles is also the son of cousin Ken Kalajian, another music maker in my life!

KATIE JEAN O'BRIEN

Who or what inspired you to start making music?

I was fortunate to have musician parents. From day one (perhaps before!), they exposed me to such a wide variety of music spanning from classical/musical theatre to jazz/pop/folk. As an only child living in a not-so-child-friendly part of town, I spent most of my days rummaging through my parents' records and cassette tapes and soaking up every bit of recorded music we had. I remember memorizing almost all of it and setting up my stuffed animals to create storylines to entire albums. During these times, my young self fell in love with Barbra Streisand, Linda Ronstadt, and any musical theatre recording we had (West Side Story being my favorite).

I also grew up being surrounded by a nurturing, very musically-oriented church family. I thrived on learning gospel music and singing in choir. It's how I really honed my harmonizing skills! To this day, singing harmonies is one of my favorite ways to sing. It's so very satisfying.

What have been the greatest joys as well as challenges thus far in your music-making?

Boy, the list is long for both! I'll start with the challenges. As you might be able to imagine, my biggest challenge was stage fright, which was a result of my insecurities and anxiety. Though I was nurtured by my lovely church family, my peers were not so kind. I was bullied like you wouldn't believe in

elementary school. I was the only student in a very poor community school who had ever chosen to play an instrument. I was made fun of on a daily basis for carrying my oboe around. It was pretty awful. I also had really crooked teeth and terrible skin, which added fuel to the fire. Funny enough, since I didn't have any friends anyway at that point and I wasn't allowed to play outside because it was too dangerous, I spent most of my free time after school practicing my oboe or recording my own voice into a cassette player and listening back!

This brings me to my joys! I used to get out all my stuffed animals and put on little musical productions to whatever musical theater recordings I stumbled across in my parents' music library. As mentioned above, I also recorded myself a lot. Sometimes I was a radio announcer or a famous singer. I even pretended to be different cartoon characters so I could hear how I could change my voice when I listened back. I started mimicking female singers that I adored: Barbra Streisand, Linda Ronstadt, and the various musical theater female leads from the likes of Les Miz and West Side Story.

I truly believe that these challenges and joys shaped me into the singer and performer that I am today. It was a long road reaching a place of confidence on stage, with all the insecurity and self-loathing I battled on a daily basis. However, I forced myself to plow through these uncomfortable situations until it got easier. This experience helps me relate to my students and aspiring singers who suffer from the same anxieties and insecurities. Because I can truly understand what they are going through, I'm able to help guide them into a safer, more confident place.

What do you consider to be the most important ideas and concepts to impart to aspiring musicians?

At the risk of sounding cheesy, right off the bat I would say: don't let your insecurities prevent you from pursuing your passion and joy. Too many of us do that too much. Some of us never figure out how to stop letting our insecurities and anxieties control us. Remember that mistakes and failures are absolutely necessary in order to grow and learn and improve. If you can just keep in mind that mistakes and failures are not negative but, rather, an exciting way to become even better at who you want to be and what you want to do, you will find the process much more invigorating and satisfying. In a way, music really is a form of therapy.

Stay the course. Keep doing what you love. Be willing to accept challenges and new ideas from other musicians and teachers. Practice is important. You may have a natural gift or something, but nothing replaces consistent practice. Most professionals practice every day for several hours. Do what you can with the time and tools you have, consistently, and you'll be amazed at the outcome. We are NEVER done!"

I met my friend Katie O'Brien in 2017 during my first interview at LB Music School. I wanted to learn more about her before our conversation and so I Googled her and found some of her music tracks online. I was so impressed by her incredible voice that the first thing I said to her was "Oh my God, Katie… you have such a beautiful voice!"… and the rest is history. She's not only Head Instructor at the music school, she performs in her own band (KTO Band) and duo (Katie O'Brien Duo). I encourage every aspiring music maker to read Katie's words of wisdom more than once throughout their career.

EILEEN PATTEN OLIVER

As far back as I can remember, music was an ever-present part of my life. My mother played piano and my oldest sister played violin. My sister especially loved all Classical music, and I grew up hearing Bach, Beethoven, Mozart and so many others, along with the 1950's Rock n' Roll and Rhythm and Blues both of my sisters loved. I had piano lessons as a child but didn't really put a lot of energy into it, a thing which I much regretted as I got older. While I can read music as a result of those lessons, I read it in much the same way as a 6-year-old might read Dostoevsky!

I was chosen to be in my school Glee Club at 9 years old which was a great honor to me as it was unheard of for a child so young to be included. Music was always important, but at the same time, drawing and painting were always on my mind. It has been my observation that most people who practice one of the arts also at least dabble in others. In my youth I balanced both fairly evenly, picking up guitar when I was twelve, mostly to accompany myself singing. At the same time, I was learning about watercolor and oil painting, the latter of which became my medium of choice. Making music began to take a back seat to making paintings by the time I was in high school. Music became the thing I dabbled in. It never went away but became something I did for my own enjoyment.

Some forty years later, music, once again, started edging out painting in my world. I got more serious about playing guitar but that was still more of a backdrop to singing, which I loved to do. I lived in Maine at the time and started performing at some small venues around the state, and played live a few times on WERU in Orland, Maine, a community radio station founded by Noel Paul Stookey of "Peter, Paul and Mary" fame. This was one of my happiest times in life, surrounded by other singers/musicians who all shared that same passion.

Life circumstances brought me back to Massachusetts from Maine, and though initially I still took my greatest joy from making music and finding so many other wonderful musical people here on the North Shore, I eventually eased back into painting. Living in a place that has the oldest art colony in the country had a lot to do with that! I'm now a full-time painter, but still enjoy playing and singing when I get the opportunity. In a different life I'm sure I would have made music more of a priority and may have even pursued it as a profession. For now, it remains something that makes life so much more enjoyable to live.

One of my favorite artists is my high school classmate and friend Eileen Patten Oliver. She is an award-winning, full-time painter today but still enjoys singing and playing guitar when she has the chance. Two of Eileen's paintings hang proudly in our home and I cherish them both. Whether she's painting or making music, her passion for the arts has been instrumental in her life. I agree with Eileen. Music does make life so much more enjoyable to live—and you can't beat that!

SAM DRAPER

Where do you practice? In the living room? Maybe in your bedroom, the hall, or if you're lucky a dedicated music room. All are fine places to practice, and ones I have spent many hours in trying to get to grips with my instrument. I have also developed a habit of practicing in slightly less obvious places.

I can include planes, trains and buses on my list, as well as the car I'm driving when at red lights. Queuing at the supermarket is a perfect practice venue as is the kitchen whilst waiting for the water to come to boil. I see no reason not to practice when in the waiting room for a doctor's appointment or sitting at your desk staring at a blank document, as I found myself doing just moments ago.

Obviously, it would be inappropriate or impossible in most of these situations to break out your guitar and start shedding your favorite licks. I cannot imagine airline passengers being happy with my practicing scales at 40,000 feet but practice is a much wider concept than a lot of people realize. I estimate that around 85% of my practice is done with the instrument and the other 15% takes place in the venues I mentioned.

Mental practice is a huge source of development for players of all ages and abilities. That difficult section that you only get right 50% of the time is perfect fodder for the mental practice practitioner. Think through the passage slowly, identifying in your mind the areas that trip you up. The section may have 50 notes in rapid succession but I suspect only a few actually cause you trouble. Identifying these notes while away from the instrument is a big step forward. When you return to the instrument you can now focus on the specific areas identified without getting frustrated at the whole passage involved.

Mental practice is also ideal for memorization. If you can remember every note, with every fingering, every breath, every dynamic change or chord change when away from your instrument, you'll find it a lot easier when you return to it. When I was doing college auditions at 17, I was on a lot of trains to distant cities in the UK. On every single trip, I played through in my mind the repertoire I was presenting.

I'm sure I drew quite a few raised eyebrows as well as I most often pretended to play the violin whilst sitting in my seat. The left hand discretely performing every shift, the right hand every bowing just as I had practiced at home a thousand times. Learning scores as a conductor also begs to be done on the bus. Just ignore the funny looks you'll get.

All my violin students will be able to demonstrate a number of exercises which I encourage them to do in class, at school, or in a dull work meeting. Small technique development exercises that go largely unnoticed but which can be hugely beneficial in the long run.

The long and the short of it, for me, is that never does a day go by when I can't practice. It may not be one in which I can get the instrument out, but if I can spend just two minutes on the bus working through a phrase then it's a day well spent.

The other type of essential practice that is done away from the instrument is listening to music. I shall be honest and say I do go through periods where I don't listen enough, and certainly to not enough new music—and my whole musicianship suffers as a result. Try to take time each week to listen to something new, and really listen to it. Even if you hate what you hear, then it is time well spent, providing you can articulate why it doesn't work for you.

One final point about practice. I've made a number of suggestions above as to why you can practice every day without fail, even if only for a few moments but I don't want to give the impression that you can only be a musician if you practice every day without fail. Some days I wake up and the last thing I want to do that day is practice. On those days, provided I don't have an important concert or session rapidly approaching, I simply don't practice. I take the day to do something else I love doing. When I return to the instrument the next day, I always feel refreshed and excited to play again.

. . . .

I met Sam in 2019 at LB Music School where he was a violin and guitar instructor during a three-month teaching assignment. It wasn't the British accent that drew me in though I could listen to Sam for hours. It was how he made each student feel at ease with his teaching style—and all the great (and often entertaining) conversations we had about music during his rare lesson breaks. I was thrilled that he wanted to share his unique perspective and advice on "practice" in this essay. If you have ever said "I don't have time to practice", read Sam's essay again!

. . . .

PATY MCDONOUGH

My mother is a lifelong musician/music educator and my father is a writer so creativity has always been in my blood. It was no surprise that during the first few years of my life, I caught the "gene" and became obsessed with music. I was the 9-year-old girl writing songs on pink construction paper during our summer trips to NH or VT, dreaming of pursuing a career in music someday (spoiler—my current career isn't in music, but my life still revolves around it.)

For me, some of the most cliché reasons for creating music ring true (maybe that's why they are so widely quoted). Music is and always has been an outlet. Whether I am listening to a song that perfectly reflects how I'm feeling that day, or writing a song because I can't find one that says what I want it to, music is always a place to turn to. More recently, I have been writing music as a way to sing the things I don't feel like I can say.

I have been particularly proud of my growth in my songwriting and piano playing over the past 5-6 years or so. However, I think like any musician and/or songwriter, the biggest challenge is self-deprecation. Usually, I am my own biggest critic. I think that's a similar feeling for artists of any kind. You are always looking to improve and find ways to reinvent either yourself or your sound, and sometimes that line gets blurred into making you think what you've created isn't "good enough".

I never had any professional background. I never ended up going to school for music. Everything I have ever written/sung has been purely by ear and because I was born with good pitch. I guess the best advice I can give anyone who is reading this is to never compare yourself to others. Believe in whatever it is that you are writing, singing, or playing. It's a good thing if you don't sound like "everybody else". That's what will set you apart. Telling a musician not to criticize themselves is like telling water not to be wet, but that's what has allowed me to write so freely these past few years. There is no such thing as instant gratification with making something. A song is not always done the same day you start it. Music has evolved and will continue to evolve, so don't be afraid to say or do something different with your own.

Lastly, especially for songwriters, write everything down. If you come up with even one line that you think will be useful someday, write it down. Record it on your phone or computer. I can't count the number of times I've written a verse or a half song and revisited it later just to end up using it in something I've since completed.

One of my favorite artists of all time is John Mayer. He is a phenomenal guitarist and songwriter. He has said many wise things about music and creating music over the years, but this is one of my favorite quotes from John that I think perfectly sums up how I feel about my own path and overall individualism in music:

"You're not here to line up behind what's cool, you're here to share what you truly love even if people aren't into it at the moment. Walk alone and gather a line behind you."

I met Paty in 2017 at LB Music School where we were both administrators. The first time I heard her sing an original composition while accompanying herself on piano, her music-making brought tears to my eyes, I was so emotionally touched. I hope someday more people will get to see and hear Paty perform. I am so grateful to her for sharing her inspiring words and valuable guidance. Her advice to never compare yourself to others and to believe in what you are writing, singing or playing is crucial for every music maker.

MIRACLE AMAH

As a child, I always loved participating in a music show or event. I found them quite fascinating, especially when it included costumes. I was in the children's choir both in church and in school and most times I got the lead in these performances because of my zeal and enthusiasm. I didn't think much about it until I finished high school and wanted to apply to college as an accounting major.

At that time, I had learned to play the violin and was practicing hard to try out for the Junior symphony orchestra at my church back in Nigeria. My church—The Mountain of Fire and Miracles Ministries, Lagos, Nigeria—has the largest musical ensembles in West Africa and my pastor Dr. Olukoya is an amazing musician and uses musical arts as a tool for youth empowerment.

As I said earlier, I didn't think much about my musical abilities because I enjoy doing it so much that I only thought about it as an extracurricular activity and not as a profession or career. By the way, not a lot of Nigerians see music as a career unless you are Davido or Beyonce. This is the reason for my ignorance regarding seeing music as a career. I have come to real-ize that this misconception is not only conceived by Nigerians but people in the world generally. And sincerely, I don't blame them for this blind spot because music is so enjoyable that it feels natural and effortless.

When people watch a performance they do not understand the amount of effort and time that has been put into it until you invite them into your world to see it for themselves. A teacher once told me: "If people can see or sense your effort on stage, then you haven't practiced enough and the music hasn't settled well in your system. Music is meant to be enjoyed and should look effortless." I would further buttress this by saying as a performer you have to enjoy the music first before your audience can enjoy it with you. Sometimes we performers get so engrossed in the art of fine-tuning our techniques and all the hard stuff, that we forget what brought us into music in the first place. And for most people, it is the euphoria we feel after listening to or performing a beautiful piece of music.

If I had one piece of advice for someone who is considering the music path either as a career or on the side, I would say, never stop having fun with it. I have had a bunch of voice students join my studio after not singing for

a while and I always ask them what their previous experiences have been and if they wanted to change something. Most times, they tell me how they get so involved with criticizing their technique and building so much tension in their voice over a period of time due to anxiety, that they finally stopped singing out of fear and frustration. I have been there and struggled for a while. However, one way I have been able to overcome these challenging times is by remembering what brought me into music in the first place and not getting so obsessed with the technicalities that I forget to have fun and invite my audience into my world.

Jonathan McReynolds is a popular gospel singer whose song "Comparison Kills" contains my last piece of advice.

One of the best decisions you can make in your life as a Music Maker is to not compare yourself with the next person in the room. No matter how talented you are, you will always meet someone whom "you think" sounds better than you or is more musical than you and you will want to compare yourself with that person's talent or progress. Please don't! As cheesy as this may sound to you, you are one of a kind. As flawed as 'you think' you are, you are unique and no one else can do what you do. I keep using air quotes for the words 'you think' because most times the limitations we have are all made up in our heads.

Sing with your heart not your head! Your head tells you all the things you can't do and how your friend can do it better than you but don't allow it. You are so unique that no one else in this world has your voice, so don't go into the practice room trying to imitate your super talented friend, voice teacher or that super star that you listened to and whose voice you love. The reason why we practice is not to sound like Michael Buble, Leontyne Price or Beyonce; it is to keep rediscovering your unique voice and to carve a niche for yourself. If Idina Menzel (from Frozen) did not find her voice, we would not know her today. Stop comparing yourself with someone else! Stop measuring your progress with someone else's! Keep practicing, stay positive, be yourself and keep having fun.

I met Miracle in 2019 at LB Music School where she taught voice and piano on short-term assignments while studying at Longy School of Music for her Master's degree in Opera and Vocal Performance. I recall how excited she was the day she learned of her acceptance in the doctoral program at James Madison University where she earned her Doctorate of Musical Arts in Vocal Performance and Pedagogy. A native of Nigeria, Miracle is an award-winning professional soprano and Assistant Professor of Voice at Bradley University—and she shares crucial advice in this essay.

TOM HUGHES

All my life, I have always been the outsider, the quiet one, the Lefty, the last one to be picked for the team.

Music has been and still is my ESCAPE. It doesn't ask me to be the best or be the same as everyone else, it forgives me for my mistakes

and allows me to express my emotions through the fretboard.

It helps me remember my Mother and Father with some old jazz tunes like "Misty" or "Autumn Leaves", two of their favorites and it stirs my emotions when I play "Amazing Grace" or "Danny Boy".

I met my friend and fellow lefty guitarist Tom at LB Music School while he was studying guitar. We loved talking about music and guitars after his lessons were over and he always had a couple of great anecdotes to share. In just a few heartfelt sentences, Tom candidly describes the emotional impact that music-making has had and continues to have on his life. Tom's not alone, that's for sure. For many of us, music is indeed our escape.

SATIK ANDRIASSIAN

Music is the only art form that can open your heart,
fill you with joy and heal your suffering.

—Satik Andriassian

Words of Wisdom from a Music Legend

When I was a young student, I had the opportunity to cross paths with Beverly Sills, one of the greatest sopranos of our time—and a person of great beauty, glamour and wisdom. During our brief conversation, I recall timidly expressing to her my doubts regarding my musical abilities. Without hesitation, she responded with these words: "There's *always* room for new talent."

As an impressionable youth, I soaked up her words of inspiration and kept them close to my heart throughout the years. They were my consolation with every setback—and my reward for every achievement.

Many years have passed since that memorable encounter but I still think about that beautiful spring afternoon at Los Angeles's Dorothy Chandler Pavilion and often wonder what mystical power brought Beverly Sills and me together on that day. The wisdom that she shared with me in those few moments has had a lifelong influence on me. I learned that having "talent" is only a starting point, an inner driving force. To become the *master* of your talent takes diligence, commitment and devotion.

My friendship with Satik began online in 2015 when she commented on my Facebook post of the 2009 video of Sharon Isbin and Berta Rojas's beautiful live performance of "Porro" at the Ibero-American Guitar Festival. We started messaging—and the rest is history. Satik teaches classical guitar at California State University, Los Angeles and is Director of the Classical Guitar Ensemble as well as the founder/director of the GOHAR AND OVANES ANDRIASSIAN Classical Guitar Competition and Festival. I have such respect for her accomplishments in classical guitar and I deeply cherish our friendship. In my next life, I will be her student! Given that we are both Armenian-Americans, I also feel like she is a special member of my family.

BETHANY HICKMAN

Prioritize authenticity.

So much of this business, this career, is a matter of chance (or divine intervention). You can present your best 100% of the time, and you still might not get the job. You might not have the right look or the right sound or even the right connections. For me, the more rejection I encountered, the more I questioned what I was doing wrong. What was it about me that people didn't like? I started obsessing over my body, my technique, my acting until I thought each was perfect. I stopped singing with any kind of conviction or feeling because my mind was consumed with the mechanics of my performance.

Throughout your career, you will work with a number of teachers, coaches, directors—all of whom will have an opinion about how you should do something. As a student, I loved being told what to do because I was really good at delivering exactly what was asked of me. But when I got out of school, I realized I had become this cookie-cutter singer. I would mold myself into what someone else wanted instead of bringing my own ideas to the table. In a career that is so subjective, you want to surround yourself with people whose opinions you trust, but more importantly, those people need to give you permission to make your own artistic choices.

At the end of the day, you're the one onstage. You're the one performing, and you know your abilities better than anyone. Every artist has something unique and authentic to bring to a role so don't sacrifice yourself trying to please someone else. First and foremost we are servants to the music, then we serve our listener, but through it all, we must honor ourselves.

I met professional singer and vocal coach Bethany in 2019 at LB Music School where she taught voice and piano while living in the Boston area. Having trained in both classical and contemporary styles, Bethany is passionate about helping singers of all genres better understand their voices and achieve their vocal goals. In addition to her private coaching and masterclasses, she discusses vocal technique in her popular YouTube channel "The Vocalyst" which she created in 2022 to make vocal pedagogy more accessible and to encourage an appreciation of artists worldwide. Last but not least, Bethany has one of the most beautiful voices I have ever heard!

JOHN M. KENNEDY

In the vastness of silence
I create,
I write,
I explore.

In the vastness of silence
I create,
I explore,
I define.

In the vastness of silence.

I met Dr. John M. Kennedy, DMA, world-renowned composer and Professor
of Music Composition at California State University, Los Angeles in
2016 through my dear friendship with Satik Andriassian (Dr. Kennedy's
beloved wife and another great music maker included in this book). An
outstanding performer on the double bass as music director of the Chamber
Players of Los Angeles, Dr. Kennedy has been recognized for his musical
achievements with numerous grants and with the CSULA Outstanding
Professor Award (2021-2022). I am honored that he wrote this poem for us.

MICHAEL AARON LEVINE

first started learning music when I was 18 and picked up the guitar. And I picked it up mostly because I thought it was cool. At the time, I was really into the kind of rock bands I'd hear on the radio—The Foo Fighters, Metallica, The Red Hot Chili Peppers, Mötley Crüe—and the punk and alternative tracks in the video games I was playing—Grand Theft Auto, SSX, Burnout, and especially Tony Hawk's Pro Skater. What really motivated me to dive deeper into music, around the end of college, was when I started going to live shows. The energy present at a live show when the band sounds great and the crowd is excited is incredible.

As I got better at playing the guitar, I started to realize that the core of what I liked about songs wasn't the brutal guitar riffs or the blazing solos; it was a bit more holistic. And I found myself gravitating toward the focal point of the vast majority of rock music (and most popular music in general): the vocals. Some people start singing as kids and are able to pick it up very naturally. Unfortunately for me, I was not one of those people. I am however, the kind of person who compulsively sings whenever I think—or at least whenever I can effectively pretend—that no one's listening. So I may as well try to get good at it.

With the help of all the many great teachers I've had along the way, whether it's for guitar or voice or writing and recording, I've found the two biggest keys to my growth as a musician have simply been practice and persistence. Progress may not always come quickly and may not even feel

apparent, but the only way to get there is to sit down and put the time in and come back to it week in and week out.

These days I've been structuring my musical learning around creating recordings. From transcribing covers to writing original pieces to learning the guitar and vocal parts, to recording and mixing, the process makes me engage with a wide variety of musical skills while also having the ability to home in on individual elements I want to focus on and practice in a given song.

Dr. Michael A. Levine is an imaging scientist who earned his PhD in Biophysics at Harvard in 2020. I met Michael in 2017 at LB Music School where he is an accomplished voice and guitar student and I therefore know him best as one of the special music makers in my life. He also enjoys writing original music, transcribing covers and creating recordings. One of my favorites is his rendition of "Say Goodbye" by Theory of a Dead Man.

MICHAEL THOMAS DOYLE

There was an old ragged T-shirt my father used to wear to my hockey practices when I was a kid. It read "SHUT UP AND PLAY" with a graphic of a puck slamming through broken glass. Boy, was he right. Maybe I'll frame that T-shirt next to my first platinum record.

——Michael Thomas Doyle

I met my friend Mike in 2017 at LB Music School where he teaches guitar, drums, bass and piano. A brilliant musician, educator and Twitch streamer, he is passionate about lighting the fire in aspiring music makers of all ages and skill levels. I have fond memories of our music chats when I was administrator at the music school. I loved it when he made lists of the guitarists I needed to listen to if I wanted to get into jazz guitar. An awesome artist in his own right, Mike enjoys playing in Kind King, an experimental musical collaboration incorporating elements of post-rock, ambient and jazz styles. I love their original tune "Apollonia".

TIM O'BRIEN

Music is art and art defines a culture. So much can be learned about a society from its music.

I come from a musical family. My mother was a concert pianist, my father had a great Irish tenor voice and played harmonica, and all my siblings could sing and play one or more musical instruments. We all learned at an early age to sing in parts so we had our own family choir. Two of us pursued music performance.

Even though my siblings and I were exposed early and consistently to musical training and appreciation, I believe that music is inherent in all of us and has a profound effect on us whether we have had training or not. From the lullabies and happy songs mothers sing to their babies to the comforting songs offered to the elderly, music has a way of affecting us through the entire spectrum of our emotions.

I am a scientist by training and understand that mathematics is the language of science but Music is the language of the soul."

I met Tim through his daughter Katie O'Brien (also featured in this collection) back in 2017 at LB Music School. He is an outstanding vocalist and has been singing in Katie's A Cappella group for many years. My favorite music-making memories of Tim are when he sings and plays guitar either as a solo performer or in a duet with Katie. I love his rendition of "Don't Think Twice, It's All Right", I get a bit teary when he sings "Cat's in the Cradle" with Katie and, as a guitarist myself, I admire his ultra-smooth fingerpicking! Most of all, Tim is a Dad who gives his all when it comes to supporting his favorite music-maker and daughter Katie O'Brien and her KTO band and duo!

WILLIAM J. BONES

Musically-Related Ramblings of a Guitarist

The Background

I was born in 1961 into a working-class family in the North West of England, the only child of a typewriter mechanic and a wages clerk. I wish I could say that I have some divinely-gifted genetic connection with music, that it was installed in my DNA, that my mother played me Mozart while I was still in her womb. But I can't.

I'm not from a musical family; I don't really remember the wireless (radio) being on much as a kid and there were not that many records in the house. The Beatles were frowned upon and the Rolling Stones were considered to be the very spawn of Satan himself.

I can, however, remember the defining moment of my musical awakening. It would have been 1965. "(I Can't Get No) Satisfaction" came on the radio and, according to my Dad, from then on that was the only tune I sang, only the first line and *that* opening guitar riff. I was hooked, sonically addicted and, unbeknownst to this small boy in short trousers, Keith Richards had aurally injected my little ears with musical crystal meth. I couldn't get enough of the stuff. "Baa Baa Black Sheep" could never again bring satisfaction to this boy, only Mick & Keith could do it for me, who rather ironically couldn't get any (satisfaction).

The Teenage Years

At the age of eleven I found myself completely lost in a system of education that I did not understand. The all-Boys Grammar School.

How I passed the exams to get there remains a mystery to me but nonetheless I was thrust into a world where teachers were called "Masters" and wore capes and of older boys who seemed to me to be giant hippies. This was 1972; long hair, peace and love were still in vogue. The upper sixth formers, who referred to each other as "man" or "dude", ran about the corridors reliving Monty Python sketches and were super cool to us lowly first formers.

"Hey man", "far out" and so on. A whole new language needed to be learned if I was going to survive. These new linguistic skills were in fact a code, words our parents could never understand, or so we thought, Daddio.

Break times and "Common Rooms" were our sanctuaries from the drudgery of pointless algebra. There was a record player for starters. Older boys would wander round with vinyl albums under their armpits, carried like flags of honour. These albums were played in the common rooms, gatherings of boys listening intently to the latest tunes on offer. Smaller boys hanging onto the wise sage-like opinions of the upper sixth formers. This was where my musical education really began.

Prog Rock and (what is in the year 2021) Classic Rock were what we listened to. A diet of Pink Floyd, AC/DC, Led Zeppelin, Yes, Black Sabbath, Rory Gallagher, Deep Purple, Roxy Music was the stuff we gorged our ears upon. The writings on the album sleeves were studied as if they were the Ten Commandments and we were their musical disciples.

Pop music was strictly a no no. Some of the more fervent common room occupants would have gleefully had the members of ABBA and their fans machine gunned in the quad. The Old Grey Whistle Test *had* to be watched and discussed in detail for the whole of the following week. Occasionally, you could borrow an album that would be taken home and played on the family record player, savoured by me much to the horror of my parents. This was the world I inhabited and I loved it, the camaraderie and belonging that music, *our music*, brought.

The Curse of the Left-Handed

I am left-handed. An inherited curse. Both my Dad and my Grandad were lefties. Some of the richer kids would bring guitars into school where they would show off newly acquired musical "Smoke on the Water" skills. After-school bands were formed. These guys, in my eyes anyway, were the coolest of the cool. Kids would queue up waiting for an actual go on an actual guitar. Me too, only to find the strings were the wrong way round and the chords they tried to show me simply didn't work upside down.

I was crushed. Left-handed guitars just didn't exist. Even Hendrix had to swap the strings over, and I had seen this on the TV with my own eyes. Get my Dad to buy me a guitar? That would have been difficult enough. Find a left-handed instrument? Impossible. Get a Fender Stratocaster? With which you could flip the strings over a la Hendrix ? I might as well have asked for a Ferrari. I was doomed and I didn't want to be a drummer.

My mate Andy (who had a guitar) and I would spend many a Saturday with our teenage noses pressed up against the music shop windows in search of the lefty guitar. It was simply beyond my horizons. I could listen to the music but would never be able to play it for myself. Air guitar sucks.

Andy and I got older and taller and went to concerts or "gigs" as they *must* be referred to. We lived a bus ride away from Manchester, a city which had both a University and a Polytechnic college. The music scene was vibrant. Through the 1970's, every Saturday night was spent at the Student Union Bar where we witnessed real live music for ourselves. It was magical, AND I had a Saturday job, which meant I had some independent money AND I managed to buy an actual guitar (a cheap Telecaster-style job) on which I could flip the strings around and play. I was in the game, no longer a spectator.

I had a lot of catching up to do. Prog rock was out; punk rock was in⊠ which was great because punk was/is super easy to play. For the first time in my life I felt cool. Music and a guitar had done that for me. As U2 would some years later have it: "three chords and the truth".

Now It Goes Downhill.

At the age of 19, I left the Grammar School and got a real job working for a High Street Bank. A career was the thing to have back then, and if you wanted a promotion, you needed some extra qualifications. This meant University study. Hard enough at the best of times but studying and homework after a full day at the office was very time-consuming and exhausting.

The Gitty was laid to rest. I still went to concerts, just not as many and I still listened to a lot of music. As for playing? The strings went rusty and so did I.

My mate Andy left for another city to study music properly, I moved around with work and we lost touch. My musical touchstone was gone and I was now living a different dream. A proper well-paid career with prospects, house, car, nice holidays. Blah Blah Blah.

Finally! Many Years On.

Lefty guitars were appearing, I would still go into the odd music shop for a mooch and there it was on the wall. A white left-handed Fender Stratocaster. The seed was re-sown. I was 39 years old and had the cash.

The following week, I returned to the store ready, willing and able to buy the Unicorn Strat, only to find it had gone. Another branch had sold it. I was gutted. But, the search was again now on for real. Several phone calls later and after several visits to music stores, I found not one lefty, but two. A brown "Made in Mexico" Fender Stratocaster and a considerably more expensive "Made in the USA" black Fender Stratocaster. No other colours were available to the lefty. Brown or black, that was it. Just as well I wasn't a fan of Hank Marvin because a red Strat was out of the question.

Eric Clapton very famously played a black Strat, so that was the thing for me. If it's good enough for Eric, then simple logic dictates it should be good enough for me. Plus, ALL of the great and the good had been pictured with a Strat at some point and that was the only endorsement I needed.

I put a fair-sized dent in the bank balance and went home with a spring in my step feeling like a teenager again. I still have my black Strat. She's in mint condition and is generally referred to as "The First Wife" (they all have names don't they?)

Should Be Easy Enough?

Shouldn't it? I mean, I've got a professional good quality instrument so why have I not got instant Eric Clapton skill levels?

Erm...in the euphoria of buying the instrument I had conveniently put aside the thoughts that the bendy, wiry stringy things hurt your fingers; that said fingers would not do what my brain asked of them and that I could only remember three chords. I had to start again.

Progress is slow, and frustrating. I seem to have fists of ham and fat sausages for fingers.

Andy Turns Up !

Many years after Andy and I lost touch, I attended the birthday party of the son of a colleague. My old school friend Andy was there!

It turns out he got his music degree and became a high school teacher. The teacher of the son of my colleague. A truly remarkable coincidence and happy days!

Andy and I arrange to meet up, catch up, chat about music and guitars.

I take the troublesome Stratocaster and my even more troublesome fingers with me and we get started with the aforementioned.

We have a weekly date to chat the nonsense that men do, drink a couple of beers, listen to the music of our youth and play guitars. In an instant warp of time we had rewound twenty years of our lives and were Grammar School Boys again, except with beer. I am consumed again with music and guitars.

My Real Musical Education

Is still a work in progress and after twenty or so years of practice, I'm still learning. I'll share some nuggets with you.

Gear and Equipment

It's fair to say that acquiring musically-related stuff, and in my personal case, *guitar*-related stuff is a habit that makes a heroin junkie seeking a fix look like a lightweight. I would read and absorb guitar magazines from cover to cover; a visit to a music store to buy a pack of strings and a couple of picks could easily take three hours while I searched the wall of guitars hoping to spot a lefty. Musos would meet in stores just to ogle the kit and preach the gospel of Gibson and Fender. I had found a new brethren and the music store was our church.

Dear Reader, try not be a gear addict. Having more guitars, more amplifiers, more effects pedals and so on will NOT make you a better player. If anything, it slows down your progress. They can be a distraction. It does however, make you a better-equipped player and if you consider that a guitar is an objet d'art then you can justify your gitty habit purely on the basis that they look nice on the stand.

More on the guitar herd later.

So, The First Wife and I are getting on quite nicely and with time my fingers possess the calluses of a seasoned pro.

Time to buy an Amplifier. So many hours of research in the magazines are needed and several trips over several weeks to the music stores.

Given that I've been to about a thousand gigs and always looked at the backline, I conclude that I must have a Marshall 100 Watt head and a 4 x 12 Cabinet. Nothing else will do. Or for Metallica fans, "Nothing Else Matters".

A sunny Saturday arrives and into the store I stride. I am now a gentleman of a certain vintage, I have the cash and amplifiers aren't bothered if you're left handed or not. Up to the sales counter I go and confidently ask the sales assistant to demonstrate the wall-of—death Marshall amplifiers they have on display. I am in my element.

The conversation does not go as I thought it might.

Sales Chap: "So where will you be playing this rig, Sir ?"

Me : "In my living room or my mate Andy's living room and in the fullness of time and with a bit more practice, perhaps the open mic night in the local pub."

Sales Chap: "I see. This amplifier is perhaps a bit...ummm ...loud... for those venues, Sir."

Me: "Nonsense! This is what the pros have. I have a black Strat, same as Eric and the Marshall 100 Watt is the perfect partner for it."

Sales chap: "I'll set it up in the sound booth for you."

Me: "Excellent."

Fifteen minutes later, I have the sound booth to myself. It's an insulated box around 12 feet square. At one end is the Marshall sitting atop a 4 x 12 cabinet. At the other end is me sitting atop a practice stool with the solitary left-handed guitar that music stores now seemed to carry in stock just in case a left-handed person turned up. For the geeks, it was an Epiphone Les Paul and actually a good guitar.

Sales chap: "I've set the volume up to around 15%, you just flick the switch from standby to "On" and off you go. Have fun!" and with that, the sales chap departs.

Me: 15% volume? **F**K OFF !** Everyone knows that to get the best out of a valve amp you have to crank it. I have read such things in the magazines so therefore it is true.

So...up to the Marshall I go and spin the volume round to a more respectable 80%, flick the switch to the "ON" position and back to my side of the room. The power hum coming from the black beast is menacing.

Sitting atop the stool, I pick up the guitar, confidently grab an E major chord and hit the strings. I was expecting that famous power amp "break up", glorious and rich harmonics, some loudness, obviously...but I got...SILENCE. I had omitted turning up the volume control on the guitar. What a buffoon.

Smug Sales chap sticks his head around the door and reminds me to turn the volume knob up on the guitar. He promptly departs. Right, here we go again. E major chord under my calluses, volume knob up fully and hit the strings.

Holy JEEEEEZUZ, the volume is properly deafening, as in I thought I had gone deaf. I was left with ringing in my ears and I genuinely did check to see if they were bleeding. But more than that, the sheer volume of the thing was reverberating through my innards. One chord was all it took. This amplifier was not for the faint-hearted and certainly not for anyone who wanted to retain some hearing.

Turn the thing off sharpish was my only thought. The sales chap returns and for the next 15 minutes I have to lip-read.

Amplifier-wise, I need a plan B.

Sales Chap brings in a small box which, judging by the knobs on it, is a guitar amplifier and places it on a chair next to the beastly Marshall. He plugs into it and plays. It sounds amazing and I can stay in the same room.

He patiently explains that whilst my theory and research were correct re: "Turn it up!", guitar amplifiers with that amount of power and volume are simply unusable in the real world unless you're going to play in a stadium. He is correct, of course, and I leave the store with a 10 watt valve amp which I played for years and which (actually) was still too loud for the living room.

So, I have a nice sounding amplifier and a professional quality guitar. So why don't I sound like Eric Clapton ?

As my old friend patiently explained to me...

"You will NEVER sound like Eric Clapton. You could plug into his rig and it will sound like you. Eric could plug into your rig and it will still sound like Eric. Tone is in the fingertips not the gear."

This is a basic truth. Most of the greats used a guitar, a cable and an amplifier. The fancy gadgets were simply not invented.

The overdrives, distortions, modulations and what-not tend to mask your defects as a player. Play without them and your technique will improve. That's a good tip.

I'm still disappointed that I can't replicate Jimmy Page note for note. More wise advice on the way. They rarely play the same thing twice, we only hear the final recorded version, and for the venues that 99% of us will ever play, if the audience can recognize the tune and sing along with it, then you've got a good result.

Reading Music?

My weekly sessions with Andy continue and I'm getting better, I'm even swotting up on some theory. When I started out, no way was I going to bother with the black dots and squiggles that resemble fly poo on music notation paper. That is definitely not rock & roll.

Andy points me towards tablature, or "tab" and I am saved. I can make sense of tab. Actual music notation still gives me the jitters!

Progress now accelerates. I can read tab and chord charts. I can play tunes.

Practice.

Personally, I prefer to practice with someone else. And it can be anyone. A singer, bass player, drummer, keyboard player. Any of them will add some context to your playing. It took me ages to figure out that the guitar is most often there to accompany the singer. That is, support the song. We need to remember where we fit in the "mix". You don't have to play all the time. The gaps in between the notes are just as important.

Meanwhile, Andy reads an advert in the local paper seeking a "George Harrison" for a Beatles tribute band. He wants the gig.

We, i.e. Andy and I, now have a bit more purpose. We practice Beatles tunes. He plays the George parts and I play the John Lennon parts. Practicing songs with the tune in the background is a great way to learn where you are in the mix and also improve your timing and rhythm.

Andy gets the gig.

Jazz and Shredding?

Musical genres ? One man's meat is another man's poison. It's probably best left at that.

But...another gem to be shared.

Chords? Learn the major chords then the minor chords, then the major and minor 7ths after that? It's Jazz! That short sentence will (I think) get you to a good 80% of popular music. Most of the early Beatles tunes were in easy chords, as were the Rolling Stones'.

What's not to like?

Shredding? That is the ability to seamlessly play thousands of notes at super-fast speeds. I can't do it. I admire the people that can; their skill and control over their digits are amazing. But, you can't hum it, and that is my personal definition of a good tune. I am content to accept my musical failings but make an inward promise to look into scales a bit more.

So now what?

We live in an age where it's never been easier to learn and discover (anything). We have online everything and I can almost guarantee that someone on YouTube will have a lesson or two about whatever you desire to learn. Social media? I have new musical friends that I found through social media and we meet up at our homes on the island of Tenerife to practice and play for the sheer pleasure of it; we chat musical stuff and drink a cold one or two. Nothing has changed; it's only slightly different. Kindred spirits.

I'm a lucky fellow in many ways. I now have some more time to tinker and noodle and I'm even luckier in that I have Karen, my supportive wife who puts up with it all.

A Last Word About the Guitar Herd

I met Carolyn (whose name is on the cover of this book) through social media; we have not met in person thus far. She is a lefty, cursed with the same defective gene as Paul McCartney and me.

I bought a guitar from her and we kept in touch. My herd multiplied and continues to do so. If you are wondering how many guitars you actually need?

Optimum = the number of guitars you currently own + 1

I am an addict and Keith Richards has a lot to answer for.

Keep strumming!

I met William in 2018 in the online group "Buy, Sell, Trade Left-Handed Guitars" when I was downsizing my lefty guitar collection to the seven with whom I've developed a close relationship! I knew from the first few witty sentences that William wrote that I was going to get a kick out of this gentleman from the North West of England! I need say no more about this fellow lefty and guitar aficionado because he tells it all right here (and in the most entertaining way!)—except that I cherish our friendship, our lefty-ness, our addiction to all things guitar and, last but never least, the wonderful lesson he taught me about how to make a proper cuppa.

ABE DEWING

A few years ago, I created a one-minute video of me singing and playing guitar for the first time ever. It wasn't great but it was a lot of fun so I decided to share it as a Facebook Story. As you know, Stories disappear within a day. I definitely thought my first effort was not post-worthy so 24 hours was a good life span for it.

But then something quite unexpected happened. I started getting alerts of likes, loves and responses. It was from classmates from every school I went to, former and current colleagues, musicians I admire, castmates from films, teammates and even acquaintances. So I listened to it again and yes, it was the same spotty performance. But the difference this time? I just sat and enjoyed the experience as if another musician shared this and I felt at peace.

I honestly still can't believe how many shows I have done over the years. I would have been just happy to have played in just one…just to prove to prove to myself I can play something in addition to classical. But this many shows? Not in a million years.

I am so grateful. Thank you to all of our audiences for showing up to see us play. Thank you for letting me know that it's not about perfection. And thank you for making me the musician I am today. I would not be here if it weren't for you. Because we all know playing to an empty room is just… well *empty*.

Side Note: I finally did post the performance on my Abe Dewing Music page. I still didn't feel comfortable sharing it because…well, one step at a time.

I met my friend Abe in 2019 at LB Music School where he taught violin, piano and guitar. Abe had a special knack for making students of all ages feel comfortable in their lessons and proud of what they had accomplished. I saw many of his students walk into their first lesson with anxiety—and after a half-hour with patient Abe, emerge triumphant with a huge smile after the lesson was over. Abe enjoys his frequent gigs and can often be seen performing live and making that violin sing and dance (sometimes on top of tables!) with the Zack Bolles Band, Crush: A Dave Matthews Tribute Band and other local bands.

PHOTO CREDIT: NILE SCOTT PHOTOS

CARLA MANISCALCO-GIOVINCO

Everyone thinks that discovering music is this big event in which everything becomes instantly clear. In some ways it is—but in others, it's a small, tiny step that helps you make huge steps towards figuring out who you are, sometimes without even knowing that is what's happening. That's what music did for me. Music showed me what I could do and what I could be.

—Carla Maniscalco-Giovinco

I met Carla in 2018 at LB Music School where she taught voice and piano to students who appreciated her upbeat spirit and motivating enthusiasm. And oh can she sing! I remember my jaw dropping nearly to the floor the first time I heard the unforgettable, heavenly voice of this amazing mezzo-soprano when she performed at her 2018 "Songs of Summer" ensemble recital at St. Mary of the Annunciation Church in Danvers, MA. Carla loves all aspects of the theater and finds production management just as rewarding as being in the singing spotlight. She also enjoys teaching in her private studio, helping aspiring music-makers to develop their talents.

SAMUEL ADENIYI

First, we acknowledge that music is a universal language that every living being (not just human beings) understands and can relate to regardless of genre, culture, or tradition. Music is graced with the ability to influence our thinking, relationship with one another, culture, and the lifestyle of individuals, society, and the world.

"Music is an essential gift of life."

I doubt if this world can survive without the help of its creator God through music.

As a versatile performer, composer, and educator, I regard music as one of my most effective mediums to express my emotions and mood, experiences, and my deepest desires, especially with the help of various articulations, dynamics, expressions, even meter, and tempos.

"Music is that catalyst that soothes the soul
of anyone no matter how hardened."

As a musician, recognizing that your God-given talent would not be enough to carry out your God-given assignment to this world and also being ready to learn and train with forbearance, tenacity, intentionality, and focus are essential elements to the success of your calling as a musician.

Being sold to but not enslaved by your dream of a successful musical career is very important because while many adversaries on that rocky path to success will challenge your why and intentions, you must remain steadfast.

Personalize your training, practice, and growth but not in isolation. Always remember that there is a standard out there you must compete with to earn yourself a place. You must assess your growth and shortcomings now and then, acknowledge and celebrate it while you eliminate every form of

discouragement that comes from comparing yourself with your colleagues in the industry, which is not healthy.

"Compete with your yesterday's best, and your musicianship today will be better for it."

Do not hurry your muscles as they learn the techniques of playing that instrument or singing. Remember that it takes a while to master a new and good habit, so be gracious to yourself. Lastly, take one step at a time, be consistent, and you will get there sooner than you thought.

What a pleasure it was to meet award-winning bass-baritone Samuel in 2019 when he was teaching voice and piano on a short-term assignment at LB Music School while studying and living in the Boston area. Samuel's musical journey began in his home country Nigeria where he worked as lead singer and background vocalist and also taught singing, piano and music theory in his private studio. He later moved to the U.S. to further his studies and career. In addition to performing opera and musical theater roles, Samuel has a long history of directing church music and leading worship. His inspiring words of wisdom shared here are instrumental for aspiring and experienced music-makers alike.

MATT MACAULAY

Both of my parents were very musical when I was young. My Dad played guitar, drums, wrote songs and was always recording something in our basement. He would set up 2 tape recorders so that he could do overdubs which I thought was really amazing. My Mom also played piano and a bit of guitar. I remember being so impressed with how she could play "Yesterday" and "Für Elise" on the piano.

The thing I take the most joy from is working on being better at my craft every day. I love listening, practicing, teaching and thinking about music all the time. The guitar is my chosen instrument but a much larger understanding of music is what I'm striving for. The biggest challenge is trying to balance that mission with the compromises that making a living demands. I'm happiest when I have the time and space to practice and create but start to get a bit lost when there are too many outside demands. Music is a life's work that it is built through daily commitment so I do my best to approach things with patience, dedication and a long-term view.

I met professional jazz guitarist and singer-songwriter Matt in 2019 at LB Music School where he taught guitar, bass and piano while living in the Boston area. I admired Matt's extensive knowledge in jazz, classical and rock guitar and was fortunate to have taken several lessons with him at the music school. I remember the first time I saw Matt perform live. He was the featured guitarist that evening in the KTO Duo, accompanying vocalist Katie O'Brien. I was in awe. He made the most complex chords and improvisation seem effortless...though I know that his commitment to daily practice contributed to the brilliant music-making I witnessed that evening.

GREG SLAWSON

I must have had an early inclination for music. I remember coming home from school one day when I was around six, in tears, begging my Mom to let me take violin lessons after they were announced at school. I started with lessons on violin, and in later years switched to clarinet, baritone horn, and oboe due to teachers, braces on my teeth, or boredom with instruments. I continued playing until college, when I became too busy with schoolwork and social life. But it was during my high school years when "music" became more than taking lessons, playing in the school band, practicing, and *reading* music.

Until then, I'd never been much of a music listener, except for a bit of top 40 or pieces I was learning to play. Then, around age 16, I started to hear about weird bands like Devo and the Residents from a crazy kid in my high school who used to jump on stage during public speaking class and wildly act out songs. I was intrigued that music could be something weird, confrontational, and exciting. I started checking out bands that were known as punk and new wave. I listened to local western Massachusetts college radio for hours each day, went to the local independent record shop after school as often as I could, and conversed with members of a local post-punk band who were Amherst College students. I soon discovered the British 2-Tone ska movement, and not long after, was hooked on reggae.

I went to my first concerts—relatively obscure punk and post-punk bands that visited from Boston and New York like DNA, the Dance, and the Neighborhoods, and reggae bands like England's Steel Pulse—while 17 and still in high school. (I was allowed to enter one club just by telling the doorman I didn't drink, which was true at the time). I even tried to adopt some of the cultural trappings of these music scenes—not easy for a 17-year-old living in a small city!

My interest in music has continued to this day—over 40 years later and counting. I did college radio for several years, discovering hundreds more bands, and went to hundreds of shows. I dabbled in other music styles I had never listened to—like country and funk—after hearing punk and new wave bands that were influenced by them like Jason and the Scorchers and A Certain Ratio. Several years later I developed an intense interest in Haitian racine (roots) music, bhangra from India (after traveling there), and jazz, which led me to try out trumpet for a bit in my 30s (the toughest instrument to play in my opinion).

Still later, I "discovered" Frank Sinatra and George Jones, buying as many of their albums I could find on reissues or in used record shops. When I was close to age 50 I took up piano, so I could play solo the songs I liked. And recently I wrote two quiz books of music trivia—1050 questions in total—and even included questions on music styles I'm not a big fan of, to expand my own horizons as well as others'.

So, what is my take on all this? What's kept me into music for so long? I actually find many, maybe even most, songs to be kind of boring. I dislike most popular music, especially its overproduction and phoniness. I was into the blues, even though almost every other music nerd is. I don't enjoy reading sheet music. I have little interest in music theory, in how to construct a song with this or that chord using this or that rule. I just want to play them! And nothing turns me off more than the idea of music as a business, a song as a product, or an artist as a tool to making money.

What I do like about music is that it can be a force. It's hard for me to sit still and take it in as you would a painting on a wall or a poem being

read aloud. Unlike literature or visual art, music is about physical movement. Unlike dance performances, live music can involve the listener in the experience. To me music is more about physical, emotional, and cultural expression than anything else—and *not* about conceited songwriters praising themselves with their brilliant lyrics nobody can understand, or concert pianists showing off how fast they can play a Chopin riff.

Music to me is about an assault on the listener, created and sent by the performer, and often returned to the performer by the audience. Maybe that's why you see people at concerts getting even more involved than they do at sporting events, in church, or when listening to speeches. Maybe that's why studies show that more parts of people's brains light up when listening to or playing music than when doing any other activity. Music involves more than speech, movement, and notes or chords on a page. It's a mental and physical force that rolls these together in your bones and your body until they explode!

What attracts me to music the most is authenticity. You can feel it in a George Jones recording. You can see it in a video of Sinatra in the studio. You can experience it in clips of early performances by the Clash, Sex Pistols, Talking Heads, or Elvis Costello. These performers were not just showing off on stage to try to get attention—they were truly possessed by the music. It was another state of mind. That explains why over the years people have spent millions to listen to the piercing whine of Hank Williams, the nasal gurgle of Bob Dylan, or the messy shrieks of Dizzy Gillespie's trumpet—they felt what the artists were doing! It saddens me that talented performers like Lady Gaga feel they have to put on a meat dress to get something across. I'd much rather pay to see a band play in front of 30 people and put it all out there!

I met Greg the very first time that he walked into LB Music School in the summer of 2017 to inquire about piano lessons. Two years later, our band Electric Thermostat was formed with Greg on keys! I really enjoy being bandmates with Greg. He brings new ideas to the band and has been instrumental in helping to bring our vision of performing in public venues closer to reality. A much-admired public school math teacher to special education students, Greg has also found the time to write his third music trivia eBook (and his second on punk rock), entitled "How Trivial Can A Punk Get?" published in 2023.

ANDRÉS AMITAI WILSON (DR. DRÉS)

What inspired you to start making music?

Some say that a name is destiny and its choice circumscribes the scope of a life. My parents were both musicians–my father is a classical guitarist and my mother is a jazz pianist, so they named me after the famed classical guitarist, Andrés Segovia.

I started on piano at six years old and took lessons once a week for eight years, but other than having a good ear, I didn't display much talent. I never practiced and I hated lessons. Then, when I first heard Slash from Guns N' Roses at around nine or ten years old (keep in mind that this was the mid-90s!), I wanted to do what he was doing. His guitar-playing was so mellifluous and lyrical. I begged and pleaded with my mother to buy me a guitar and told her that having that instrument would make me practice. Finally, when I was 13, I received my first guitar.

Although a classical guitarist, my father loved Jimi Hendrix, Eric Clapton, and B.B. King. He taught me the pentatonic scale and some basic blues riffs to practice and I just couldn't stop practicing! I started learning the classic rock that my father loved and the alternative rock to which I listened as a teenager, but I steadily progressed to more difficult styles and virtuosic players like Steve Vai, Joe Satriani, and Eric Johnson.

When I got to music school at the Berklee College of Music, I studied jazz guitar but also played in progressive rock ensembles. My inspiration is and continues to be my instrument. I studied voice, piano, bass guitar and trumpet in music school and can play a bit of oud (the Arab lute) as well. But my relationship to music continues to evolve based on my love of the electric guitar. Twenty-five years after I picked up the instrument, I find there is always something to learn, and I still don't play the way I truly want.

What have been the greatest joys as well as challenges thus far in your music-making?

The greatest joy in music-making has been simply sitting with my instrument and working on something challenging with a metronome to reinforce solid time. Even if I don't get it, I take great joy in trying to stretch and evolve as a player. Playing an instrument is a Sisyphean practice that you can take through your entire life because you're never done. You're never as good as you want to be and that is what makes it fun.

My greatest challenge has been in making a steady living doing music. At first, I focused on original music and made my own albums, of which I was very proud. I moved from my native Boston to New York City after college, pushing hard by playing in clubs several times a week and seeking success, that never really came as an artist. This was demoralizing and made me take a long break from music and pursue a second career as an academic (I actually garnered a Ph.D in literature), which was just as impractical as a music degree (ha!). But later I came back to music through my love of guitar. I found great joy and made a decent living out of playing as a sideman for other artists, playing guitar for theatrical productions, weddings, functions, and teaching music.

What do you consider to be the most important ideas and concepts to impart to aspiring musicians?

Find a style that you love, listen to it, and practice as much as possible. There isn't any specific style or song that you have to learn; just do you! Nevertheless, practice deliberately, and preferably with a metronome. Five to ten minutes of focused practice every day is better than two hours of noodling once a week. Find the players that you love, learn their stuff, and copy them relentlessly until you develop your own sound.

A great teacher I once had told me that musicians are athletes and our most important muscles are our ears. Actively listen to music with the goal of learning the sounds that you love. And lastly, if you don't love learning the instrument, there is no point, but maybe you love music and have chosen the wrong instrument. Experiment with all the instruments and sounds that intrigue you.

. . . .

I met Andrés Amitai Wilson, Boston guitarist, songwriter, poet and PhD in Comparative Literature, in 2019 at LB Music School where he taught guitar and piano in several short-term teaching assignments. Andrés enjoys a busy schedule of solo and duo function gigs and as a sideman touring with Asia Mei. His début album, the blues-based Ink & Sound (2006) was named one of Boston's top five by *Metronome Magazine* in 2007. When not making cool music, Andrés aka Dr. Drés is an English, music, and yoga teacher at the Roxbury Latin School in Boston. There are so many golden nuggets of wisdom in Andrés's interview. Perfect prescriptions for aspiring music-makers!

. . . .

DAVID ZANGER

Why The Hell Do I Play Guitar?

In my first attempt to explain why I am struggling to learn to play guitar, I wrote a long essay about me, my life, what I have been through, and how that got me into the world of music. I ultimately dropped that draft for two reasons.

First my life story is, well, rather personal to me. If we're good friends, and we're sitting in my living room talking after enjoying a dinner together, I'm happy to tell you my whole life story. But given who may be reading this—from people I know a little and am friendly with, but not close friends with, to people I've never even met—you'll have to get to know me much better to hear those stories.

Second, it took forever to get to the answer. And honestly, you don't need to read about my learning multiplication in third grade to learn why I play guitar. So let's get straight to the answer. Why do I struggle so hard to learn to play guitar? Because it is the hardest thing I have ever done, and I believe that a person learns a lot more about themself by struggling toward some goal they may never reach than by doing something that comes quickly or easily and teaches them very little along the way.

Feel free to stop reading here. You've got my reason, and you can decide whether or how to put it into your life. If you want a little more detail, read on.

Life has been a very mixed bag for me—some great stuff, some terrible. I learned an awful lot getting through the nightmares, but they're not relevant here. Elementary and high school were very easy for me, MIT was the best four years of my life, I really enjoyed learning law at the University of Chicago, editing the Law Review was easy enough, clerking was great, and being a lawyer was a ton of fun.

But the place where I did my most struggling and learned the most about myself, others, and the way the world acts around me was in my martial arts training. I started in high school and kept training for the next 25 years. Class was a two-hour physical nightmare. From the moment we bowed to the instructor until two hours later, we were moving—fast. The only rest we ever got in class was either a "back rest" (lie on your back while we do some hellish abdominal exercise), or a "front leaning rest" (push-ups; typically, 100). Black belt tests were really fun. There are different ranks of black belt, and every black belt of every rank was required to take either an exam to be promoted or an "evaluation" (joke: they were exactly the same thing) at least every 2 years. Exams were about 12 to14 to 16 hours long. Not a consistent 12 to 16 hours mind you. It was about 2 hours of nonstop kicking or punching or blocking or sparring with the master's home students or whatever else the masters judging the exam wanted to see, followed by about a 2 or 3 minute "break" to go to the bathroom, or throw up, or drink as much water as you could, followed by another 2 hours of non-stop movement or whatever the masters wanted to see, followed by another 2-minute break . . . . I never knew what time the tests ended—I was way too far gone by then to read a clock.

The point of a black belt test (or evaluation) was not to see how good you were. If you weren't good enough, you wouldn't be wearing a black belt in the first place. The point was to show you how much more would be expected of you if you did get promoted. I knew a number of people who would take the test, and then quit. They were done with martial arts. They were not willing to put in what the next rank would require. I was. That was the basis around which the rest of my life flowed.

Then (there's always a "then" in any good story), I had a medical...issue (unrelated to martial arts in any and every way) . . . that, despite my numerous attempts to re-enter martial arts, made it clear that I could just not go back. My life wasn't over, but for a couple of years, it was relaxed, and I just spent a lot of time with my wife, or reading, or doing things with her and her son from her first marriage. But I was missing that "core" that made up a large part of me.

Then (second then), a music school opened up just down the street from my house. I had tried guitar before but left after a short time because I thought I really had no time for it, nor did I have any musical ability. But now I certainly had the time for it, and hey, Beethoven was deaf when he wrote his Ninth Symphony (maybe not completely deaf, but he did have to saw the legs off his piano to "feel" the song and the beat.) And some people consider his Ninth Symphony to be, well, OK.[1] So maybe...

I'm clear that I'm an extremely poor musician. I'm not looking for any sympathy here. It's just a fact. And I know that I will never play as well as Eric Clapton or Eddie Van Halen or Roy Orbison or Randy Rhoads or Stevie Ray Vaughn or Tommy Thayer. And let's definitely not forget B.B. King. So if I'm nowhere near as great as many of the greats of the guitar are or were, and I really cannot play even as well as most guitar students, why do I struggle through the six-string nightmare (and occasionally the 12-string nightmare) that is guitar. That is precisely why.

---

1 To be honest, here, I have to admit that Beethoven's Ninth is fabulous. It is way beyond magnificent. It is so fantastic that it transcends the word "music." My God, it is sound perfected. That's what I really meant when I said it was "OK."

Because it is the struggle and the effort and the failures and the repetition and the tiny, slight advancements you occasionally make that teach me about myself. And that makes the effort all worthwhile for me.

Anyone who knows my guitar-loving friend Dave Zanger is probably familiar with his sheer brilliance, generosity, compassion and unique sense of humor! I met Dave in 2017 at LB Music School where he was a guitar student and I was administrator. He would arrive early for his weekly lessons and stop by my desk to say hello and within seconds he would regale me with anecdotes that triggered side-splitting bursts of laughter. This is how we got to know each other each week. As funny as he can be, Dave is also no stranger to the serious curveballs that life can throw at you out of the blue. Thanks to his perseverance and resilience, he has thankfully hit most of them out of the park.

JANE PARK

Who or what inspired you to start making music?

My mother is a piano teacher, so she had me start violin lessons quite young. At that age, I was not aware that I was doing anything special, so there was no real awareness or feeling of inspiration. Looking back at my childhood, listening to music was an activity in my family. When one of my brothers bought a new album, we would play it on the family CD player to sit and listen to it. Again, because I was young and grew up this way, I was not aware of the musical foundation I was being given.

What have been the greatest joys as well as challenges thus far in your music-making?

The greatest joy in music making is being able to perform with other people. I think being on stage is an important and empowering feeling. The energy that an audience gives you—you can truly feel that and give it back. For me it's the process of rehearsing, getting to know my fellow collaborators, and figuring things out together that I find truly joyful. I find myself to be more process oriented than goal oriented, and I love seeing how a piece of music can change shape over time.

As for challenges, there are many challenges personally and more general. One of the biggest challenges for me was transitioning into adulthood as a musician. After graduating from college, I was quite aimless, so making

money and continuing to play the violin was very challenging. I had several periods where I thought I had decided to quit, but I could never make it a whole year without picking it back up. I had to accept that a part of me really loved to play, and that I needed to figure out how to fit playing violin into my adult, money-making, life. On paper and in hindsight this might sound very simple, but for me it was a painful process that required a lot of reflection on my part.

What do you consider to be the most important ideas and concepts to impart to aspiring musicians?

I think one of the most important things a musician does is to listen to music. It's helpful if you're a fan of that music, but it's important to listen to other genres, too. Be curious about the different parts and sounds in music, then eventually you have this feeling within you, like you want to create that sound. These days, it is the biggest motivation in my music making.

I met Boston-based American songwriter Jane in 2017 at LB Music School where she was a well-loved and respected violin and guitar teacher. I have fond 2018 memories of seeing Jane "live" in two very different musical contexts: her impressive violin performance of Robert Schumann's Sonata No. 2 for Violin and Piano accompanied by Robert Congdon at The Green Room and her Poor Eliza performance promoting her EP Ghost Town in The Burren Backroom Series (both in Somerville, MA). Jane is also the creator of Asian Glow, a performance series for the Asian diaspora in Boston featuring creatives whose genre or style doesn't necessarily link to their ancestral identity.

TIM BOURQUE

find the world of music to be an amazing world with its own unique language. Embedded within this language there seems to be an endless supply of melodic dialogue and rhythmic progression.

It's a sort of mystical language that comes from the mind of the individual. In my opinion, the world of music is something that can be truly defined as limitless and without boundary.

I met my friend and bandmate Timmy in 2017 during my first year as administrator at LB Music School where he is a guitar student. A founding member and talented lead guitarist of Electric Thermostat, Timmy has been our "rock" helping us to keep it together through our various lineup changes. Even-keeled and encouraging at all times, Timmy is always open to new musical directions and is a true pleasure to play with.

MICHAEL SCRIMA

'm not reinventing the wheel by passing on the quote "Love what you do" but I can let you know how I have personally interpreted it in my life of music.

That may seem like a command or some wisdom that suggests you can control what you care about. Neither of those is how I take it. The older I get, the more I see its value as an acknowledgement that the present moment isn't being missed when I know I'm making music that I'm happy about. If the end game becomes the primary focus, especially to those who have greatly clarified their goals as I have, too many good moments aren't going to be lived while they are happening. They'll end up as post-enjoyment if captured on a recording...and that's if you're lucky.

I've wanted to make my sole occupation a writer/performer of original music for decades. By achieving that, distractions could be set to a minimum and most of my life would be spent filled with what I want instead of what I'm just doing as a means to an end. But what good is all that goal-reaching if I'm not mentally there for it?

I took so much for granted in my teens and 20's. One of these things was the "given" that there would be people readily willing and available to join projects with me. The family-making, the house-buying, etc. are diminishing these chances among my peers. I've sworn a life of having no children and owning no property for the sake of focusing on my music. But because I set out to make music WITH others, I can't be the only one with this frame

of mind. Had I known how much more difficult it would be to find cohorts, I would have taken things more with a grain of salt among the people I made music with back then instead of ditching them. I ended up letting too much other non-musical stuff matter. I needed a thicker shell faster than I developed one. I guess that's the curse of artists in general though... too much sensitivity. It wound up overshadowing the great music we made together and my focus was on the wrong thing.

I've lost a lot of friends by being in bands with them and pushing too hard. My drive has still not been matched by any of the dozens of musicians I've worked with and it ends up making the relationships sour. If I focus on the numerous failures, I become uninspired and produce nothing.

Now here I am in my 40's no closer to what I set out for at the start. I've never been good at the game but throughout all that's happened, I'm still becoming a better musician and the last feeling of fulfillment was not that long ago. It was a simple vocal recording a couple of weeks back. But these days I can be there for those moments. The physicality of doing it, the adrenaline of being warmed up and executing well, and the proudness of an original idea are all witnessed this time around. I'm there without that past and without the future I desperately pine for.

I just let myself love what I do and at that moment, I need no plan.

I met Mike in 2017 at LB Music School where he taught all levels of piano. During my chats with Mike when we were both at the music school, he was always candid about his music-making goals and would often express the thoughts expressed here. I admire Mike for being so open about his feelings and I am so happy that he can finally let himself be in the moment, loving what he's doing while making music. Hopefully, Mike's candor will inspire others to do the same and not let worrying about the "endgame" prevent them from enjoying the "good moments".

RACHEL MORGAN

As a young girl in church choir, I vaguely remember getting a little too close to the microphone. Little did I know that for many years after that, my choir director would tell me to back up a little bit because I was always too loud. For the most part, nothing really came easy to me except for singing and because I thoroughly enjoyed it, I stuck with it. Whether it was for choir, a school play, community theater, or high school chorus, singing was something I didn't really have to work at; I didn't know how to read music, but at the time, that did not matter. I went to a Catholic school and although I would not trade that education for anything, we were never taught how to read music or play an instrument. If I could change anything, I would have learned how to do both at a much younger age.

I wasn't in the best place in my early young adult years and gave up singing for quite a while. I still appreciated music and listened to a lot of Pandora but I just didn't have it in me to sing. Years later, my choir director welcomed me back with open arms and although I continued to struggle emotionally, I hung in there. I eventually decided that I wanted music to be my main focus and started taking voice lessons. Although I stuck with voice lessons, life got in the way. Music could *not* be my main focus but I accepted that.

Singing has been a healthy release for me and without it, my emotional health tends to suffer. This past year, I have not been able to sing very much due to health issues, but I decided to learn piano to still have a musical outlet. I was fortunate to have a voice teacher who also teaches piano. Because I typically practiced my singing on my way to work in the morning, finding the time to practice piano has been a little bit of a challenge. Although it's rare, the times when I am able to practice for at least an hour are the greatest. I feel a great sense of accomplishment.

Over the course of my musical journey, I have made some great friends and I have regained a lot of the confidence that I lost as a young adult. Whether it was performing at a recital or supporting a friend at one of their gigs, I was forced out of my comfort zone and I am very grateful for all of those experiences. If it weren't for my encouraging, loving choir director and amazingly talented and supportive voice teacher, I probably would not have the passion for music that I have. Without their support and guidance, I honestly don't know where I would be right now.

One thing that I have learned is that music is always there for you no matter what. It's like a friend that you have on speed dial who's there for you whenever you need them. You can take a break and music will still be there. It will be there for you when you are isolated and lonely during a pandemic. It has given me a great sense of comfort and consistency during isolation.

It's going to take me a while, but I hope to one day bring comfort and joy to people as a music therapist. You can pursue music as a career or a hobby. You can sing every day or you can practice once a week. As long as it is something you enjoy, keep doing it. When things get tough, see it as a challenge and persevere. Enjoy your journey and do your best to not compare your journey to others which has always been a weakness of mine. You don't have to be a successful musician for music to be the most meaningful part of your life. If it's something you want to do, don't wait. The earlier you start, the better, but it's never too late to learn.

I met my friend Rachel in 2017 at LB Music School where she is a voice student and member of Katie O'Brien's A Cappella group. Music has played such a strong role in her life and singing, in particular, has been instrumental in helping her stay emotionally healthy. I always enjoyed seeing her perform at the music school recitals and admired her passion and courage in getting up on that stage and singing solo. There are so many insightful and inspiring words of wisdom in Rachel's essay and I am so grateful that shared them with us.

JULIE PERRON

Ten minutes per day will get your skills going way faster than a solid one hour per week.

Scales and exercises (vs "just learning songs") dramatically increase your ability.

Learning a new instrument grows your brain by creating new connections!

You'll never regret learning to read music. Can you imagine never learning to read, and all that would be locked away to you if you couldn't read? Yes, you need to practice reading music to gain the skill just like your 1st grade teacher had you practice reading skills every day, and now look at you!

There's a whole world of music out there. Don't limit yourself by only listening to one or two genres.

"Classical" western music will give you so much. Don't prejudge. It does take more than one listen to understand it but all you need are your ears.

Did you ever notice how simple catchy songs draw you in at first but then you get real sick of them pretty fast? That's because when you really listen, you get to know the music, and once you know it really well you become

PHOTO CREDIT: DAWN HUBBARD

bored with it. It just seems repetitive. I love and greatly respect Bobby Mc-Ferrin and I'm happy for him that "Don't Worry Be Happy" made him lots of money, but I'll be ok never hearing that tune again. He is so talented so please check out his other stuff.

Take as many opportunities as you can get to play—and play with others, especially if they're more accomplished than you. This is music education on steroids!

I studied guitar with Julie for six years starting in early 2011 at her Wood & Strings studio in Arlington, MA. She is the teacher who introduced me to classical guitar. I remember how excited I was to buy my lefty La Patrie Concert Classical guitar and begin learning with Julie who taught me the basics from scratch. To this day, I still pick up my Christopher Parkening lesson book and practice. Fluent in many genres, Julie is an outstanding teacher and musician. I am so grateful for the advice and words of wisdom she shared with us here. They remind me of how much I miss my lessons with her!

ALAN TAUBER

As a music teacher and performing musician for over 50 years, I've learned a few things. One is that enjoying music is pure fluidity and acceptance of sounds and experiences; expected sounds burning and shaping, pouncing or dramatically producing each tone you play and/ or listen to. Obviously, music is not what's written on paper or LED screens— even the music of the western world that's 200-400 years old isn't ever played the same way twice. This is because we are human, and especially in groups, teams or bands of humans there are so many variances. And THAT's what makes us FEEL the music we hear or play.

When I landed in Guinea, West Africa at the feet of my drumming master, Famoudou Konaté, it was 11 PM under a quarter moon, and I felt a presence next to me. As we gazed upwards to the dimly lit sky, he said quietly in French, "The moon is beautiful, isn't it?" And I responded, "Oui." A moment later I knew he was gone into the night. The magic had already occurred and a seed was planted. I really felt different. My friend asked, "Was that Famoudou?"

Next morning, drum class 101!

I had met the man who was to be my master for the next 20 years: the man and the music that would change the very concept and feel of music and my hearing/listening/understanding of it (or not). He shaped the way I played—and later, taught these things—every day for two decades. Famoudou changed my life, and the lives of thousands of drummers, dancers and singers. A true master in any field can transport the student to places never before visited. I try to do that very thing with my own students whenever I get the chance. Some understand, but most don't seem to grasp it, so I keep modifying my teaching abilities to reach everyone.

My father was a physician, and more than anything else in the world, he wanted me to become a physician too. But I became a musician instead, and through music I became a healer. So in a way, maybe I've accomplished more than my father expected, I'm not sure. I am sure I am grateful to all of my students for being my students, and to all of my teachers for giving me their time and teachings.

Remember: there may be many masters in your life, so learn from them all. Other sources that can apply to being inspired to play better may be a loved one, trees or the ocean. Love it all and express it on your instrument.

Maybe ALL human emotion can be felt within music and enhanced by it, as they are the same thing. Our intent, on whatever level of consciousness, is a push to explore a connection with a listener for a desired result. It's simple, really, as we are communicating from very base emotions to more complex forms, to other forms that were created to be challenging to play and sometimes hard to understand or like.

It can take a lifetime to warm up to some musical forms. That will change as our ability to really listen develops along with our playing skills. Personally, I like all kinds of music, but I still have my preferences. As we age, we may not be able to play as fast or smoothly as a young person, or be able to express the intensity available to youth, but we can accept other music easier and with more understanding as we have experienced more of life's gifts of organized sound. Now, back to the music...

And this is even more true of African drumming music, which was never recorded in any kind of written notation. Rather, this musical tradition was communicated purely by ear and by memory alone, handed down in a living chain from one generation of djembe masters to another in remote villages and coastal towns of West Africa. I have always tried to seek out and remain true to the most authentic traditional sources, so I could pass these along to my students.

My high school classmate Alan is a gifted percussionist, musician, facilitator and educator who has spent over 40 years sharing his passion for drumming and healing with the worldwide community. In 1990 he established DrumConnection, New England's largest hand drumming school located near Boston in Arlington, Massachusetts. He put a lot of thought into these inspiring words that apply to both aspiring and experienced music-makers.

KEN ROSS

Any piece of writing short of a full book or autobiography is challenging to write about my love and appreciation for music. But given the purpose of this book, and my relationship to Carolyn, who I also know would be hard-pressed to condense all her love of music into just one essay, I'd like to take this opportunity to talk about something that I think is important for new and seasoned music makers today.

And that's that music is the practice of what amounts to super-human self-patience. And maybe that's confusing to some of you. And I'll try to explain what I mean by that without getting too new-agey or celestial, because I know Carolyn will roll her eyes when she reads this and likely edit me out of her book (only kidding; I know she would never do that!). So what I mean, by "super–human self-patience," is that in the practice of music, you will have to put your amusement for the process over your contentment in the results.

There simply isn't a way that anyone has gone about learning music that hasn't required them to sit and loop the part of a difficult excerpt one hundred times or play scales at quarter speed just to get the fingerings right. These time–intensive and universally humbling experiences are what are key to becoming any sort of successful musician. And I don't think I really need to say this to most people probably reading this book who have been studying music for more than a year or two or have been around the block with these kinds of concepts. But I think it is worth re-phrasing it here, as we can all see how the world around us is becoming increasingly more focused on results and productivity.

And the performances that you see from your favorite musicians on the internet and on your favorite records are just the tip of the iceberg.

See if you can incorporate this "super-human self-patience" into your practice. Maybe it's those scales you've been trying to get together; if so, focus on the expression instead of the tempo. Or if it's a tough piece you're trying to incorporate, just kick back with some free improv. You get the idea. If you can truly relish the process, it will bring you more contentment in the end.

Ken Ross is a multi-instrumentalist and composer/producer who writes and records his own original music. I met Ken in 2018 when he taught guitar and piano at LB Music School. He was also the Band Director of Electric Thermostat, a band in which I play guitar and occasionally percussion. Ken went above and beyond as our band director (he even played drums for us back then when we had no drummer) and taught us the importance of band etiquette when the band was only a year old. To this day, my bandmates and I practice that etiquette with a high level of mutual respect.

TIM BARNARD

D on't be afraid to make "mistakes". Play the "wrong" notes, play out of time, play loud when you're "supposed" to play quiet. In this chaos, you will find your own musical voice. Don't worry about better vs. worse, only about what you can offer that is different from the rest. So make the mistakes, play with confidence, and have fun!

This is great advice from my friend Tim, a guitarist in Absurd Condition, an instrumental, progressive metal band created by Chris Savarino and based out of Long Island, New York. Tim was one of my guitar teachers at LB Music School in 2022 and introduced me to jazz guitar. I was so excited to play my first improv piece "Autumn Leaves" at the music school recital. He was also the Band Director of Electric Thermostat for one season—and directed and produced our 3-song Virtual Performance set and post-show live Q&A during COVID.

How to Order

Please see my webpage

gothamprinting.com/book/instrumental-passion

for more information.

Contact Information:
Carolyn Zeytoonian, Author
carolyn@instrumentalpassion.com